NELLIE STONE JOHNSON

NELLIE STONE JOHNSON

THE LIFE OF AN ACTIVIST

David Brauer

Ruminator Books
Saint Paul, Minnesota

This publication was supported in part by a grant from the Open Society Institute. We would also like to thank the following contributors, whose assistance we gratefully acknowledge:

Minnesota State University Student Association, Inc.; Hotel Employees & Restaurant Employees Union Local 17; Outagamie Charitable Foundation, Inc.; Marquette Banks Educational Financing Center; Minnesota AFL-CIO; Affinity Plus Federal Credit Union; Inter Faculty Organization; Minnesota State University, Mankato; Winona State University; AFSCME Council 14; AFSCME Local 4001; Twin Cities A. Philip Randolph Institute; Tamrat Tademe; Morris J. and Debra L. Anderson; Craig M. Ayers; David M. Heins; Robert C. Johnson; Jason, Elsbeth, and Anna Ross; Kyle L. Markland; Russ Stanton; Frank X. and Pennie L. Viggiano; Nicole Farber; Bernard L. and Phyllis A. Brommer; Robert O. Erickson; John J. Kaul; Andrea Ruesch; Thomas W. and Ardis L. Wexler; and Mary Stanton.

Published by Ruminator Books Press
1648 Grand Avenue
Saint Paul, MN 55105

ISBN: 1-886913-46-3
LCCN: 2001-130155

10   9   8   7   6   5   4   3   2   1
First paperback edition, 2001

Cover photo © 1999 by Doug Knutson
Cover design by Randall Heath
Book design by Wendy Holdman
Typesetting by Stanton Publication Services

Printed in the United States of America

Contents

The Good Fight

Steve Perry

The first I heard of Nellie Stone Johnson was a voice on the telephone, summoning me to meet. "I like the things you've been writing," she said. "I think we ought to have lunch." Well. Whoever this woman was, I thought, she was not exactly a kibitzer. I was then the recently appointed editor of the weekly Minneapolis alternative newspaper *City Pages,* and as a relative newcomer to the lore of Minnesota politics, I had never heard her name. But something in her tone precluded my saying no. So a lunch date was made, and then another.

Before long we were speaking several times a month. Nellie would phone, sometimes from the sewing shop she still operated on Nicollet Mall in downtown Minneapolis and sometimes fresh from a meeting in which she'd found it necessary to go upside the head of a state legislator, to discuss one of the dozen or so campaigns she was waging at any given time. Today her subject might be the perfidy of the NAACP and the Urban League, organizations she had helped build only to watch them grow fat and conservative; tomorrow it would be her rearguard fight against the governor's efforts to weaken the state Board of Higher Education, on which she served. I came to know her well enough to realize that scarcely a day of her life went by that was not principally consumed with politics and public affairs. She was eighty-five years old at the time.

Nellie Stone Johnson's public life has contained more facets than this brief foreword—or, indeed, this whole book—can fairly encompass. Her story sums up, probably better than any other, the rich if largely forgotten history of twentieth-century Midwestern radical-ism, beginning with her political baptism through the distribution of Nonpartisan League pamphlets as a young girl. Arriving in the city, she found a job as elevator operator at the Minneapolis Athletic Club—and proceeded to unionize the place, on the sly and at consid-erable risk to herself. During the cataclysmic labor struggles of the 1930s, her family trucked in produce from its farm to feed the isolated and besieged strikers; and when the radical Farmer-Labor Party was finally taken into the Democratic fold in 1944, she was on the com-mittee that oversaw the merger (at the ripe old age, I should mention, of thirty-nine). This last endeavor did not yield everything she had hoped, as she will candidly admit.

Later at night, following a couple of after-dinner brandies, she will say as much of virtually all the battles she has fought. Racism in America, she will tell you with a hard sigh, is more virulent now than at any other time in her life. I have often thought how bitterly ironic it must be for her to watch all the rollbacks, the canting betrayals of hard-won gains in civil rights and labor, that have marked the past twenty years. This is not to suggest that Nellie feels her efforts have been in vain—the furthest thing from it, in fact, and therein lies the most valuable lesson I have learned from my dear friend and mentor.

Once, when I was going through a particularly black streak of de-pression, Nellie took me to dinner. How did she do what she did? I wanted to know. How did she keep going? Where did she find spiri-tual sustenance in those times when the defeats outnumbered the vic-tories? "Well," she said finally, in a voice stern and tender, "I never saw much in God or the church, if that's what you mean. I could never un-derstand looking to the next life when there was so much to be done in this one. I get discouraged sometimes, sure. But I guess it always seemed to me there was nothing to be done but pick yourself up and go on. Maybe you wanted something more profound, but I don't know anything more profound. You've got to go on, that's all. And that's how you find such rewards and satisfactions as you're going to find, in the going on."

I have never known anyone else remotely like Nellie. If there is a particular public figure to whom she invites comparison, it is perhaps Eleanor Roosevelt. Like Mrs. Roosevelt, she is tough, kind, canny, indefatigable; and she is cut from cloth that we no longer seem capable of manufacturing: the truly public person, for whom the welfare of the many is a question more real and more important than the dramas and trials of the private, personal life. ("You know," she said once when I pressed her for personal details to flesh out a profile that I was writing, "I don't really remember. Why don't you say there hasn't *been* a personal life?")

I have only one complaint about Nellie: in the nine-plus years that I have known her, she has never once allowed me inside her home. "It's too cluttered," she'll say, demuring. "All this paper from the things I'm working on." What a glorious mess it must be, and what a contrast to the way she keeps house emotionally. "I'm not a religious person myself," says her friend and protégé, the Minneapolis civil rights activist Ron Edwards, "but I believe that if you're at peace with yourself, there are amazing things you can do. You have resilience. You have a strength no one can give you, because your soul is not in conflict. Nellie Stone Johnson's soul has never been in conflict with her principles. That's what keeps her going."

Preface

I had to be auditioned by Nellie Stone Johnson to write this book. Anyone who has faced her knows she can be a formidable presence. As a political journalist in Minneapolis, I had interviewed Nellie a few times over the years, but didn't really know her. I knew I was not black, a woman, a union member, a radical, in my nineties, or a legend. How was I going to get this woman to relate to me?

Before my screening, I tried to mentally reorganize my brain's index cards, moving what I knew of those groups toward the front. When I met Nellie at the New French Café—her favorite caffeine supplier, near her downtown Minneapolis high-rise—she was gracious, and then she crossed me up immediately.

"I want to know one thing right off the bat," she said, after firmly shaking my hand. "How well do you understand the farm?"

Farm. I wasn't prepared for this. I was from Iowa, I blurted, not really a farmer, but I grew up reading about the farm economy in the *Des Moines Register.*

"OK," she interrupted mercifully. "I just want whoever writes this book to understand how important the farm is to me. It's a very important part of me. It's where I'm from."

She immediately launched into an anecdote about her good Irish Catholic farm neighbors in Dakota County, how she felt so akin to them in class and how racism was barely a consideration, and I was hooked. We shared one of those two-hour lunches that fly by in what feels like fifteen minutes, and the surprises just kept tumbling out.

My only regret is that, not wanting to presume I had the gig, I had left my tape recorder at home.

The first question you get from friends when you tell them you're profiling a ninety-something woman is, "Is she all there?" Oh, yes. Nellie's only concession to age during our months of interviews was stamina. Don't mistake that for a lack of tenacity. At several points in the project, I ducked away for other assignments, but Nellie would always call, demanding an update. My caller ID has her name and phone number permanently burned into its LEDs, and I know now why few union recruits escaped when she was on an organizing drive.

A note about this book: occasionally, I have relied on outside interviews to augment what Nellie told me. Sometimes, others asked more knowledgeable questions, as was the case in a remarkable interview with Nellie by labor and radical history experts Rhoda Gilman, Carl Ross, Sal Salerno, Hyman Berman, Peter Rachleff, and Deborah Miller for the Minnesota Historical Society's Twentieth-Century Radicalism Oral History Project. People sometimes simply got better versions of Nellie's stories than I did, as Steve Perry, the best radical writer in the Twin Cities today, proved frequently in his 1991 cover profile for *City Pages*. I also found helpful Louise Mengelkoch's 1986 article in the *Minnesota Women's Press*. Only Nellie's quotes were used from these pieces; thanks to all the authors for so generously agreeing to let them be incorporated into her story. I also want to thank Dr. Robert L. Carothers, Nellie's dear friend, for permitting us to quote his evocative poetry.

This book does more than chronicle Nellie's life—it will hopefully add to her legacy: all royalties will go to the Nellie Stone Johnson Scholarship Fund. The scholarship Nellie inspired has helped more than one hundred students from union families attend the Minnesota State College and University system in the past decade. Many of those who sustain the scholarship made this book a reality: Tom Triplett, Frank X. Viggiano and the Minnesota State University Students Association, and Minnesota's labor movement. They all have my gratitude.

However, my special thanks go to this project's linchpins, publishers Pearl Kilbride and David Unowsky of Ruminator Books. I tortured them and they did not respond in kind.

My publisher's patience was topped only by that of my wife, Sarah, and son, Ian—I now know how incredible solidarity really is. I also know why writers so often dedicate books to their family.

Finally, to Nellie, who patiently taught her story to another neophyte, who tolerated human frailty a hundred times, and who proved her humanity by trusting someone whose life is so outwardly different from hers.

NELLIE STONE JOHNSON

Chapter 1

Family History

I have not gotten along with some writers who tried to work with me before because they always wanted to turn my story into something amazing to fit their preconceptions, like we had to overcome prejudice every day. The truth is, growing up, we were a normal family, a hardworking bunch, and we were treated like a normal family. No one these days wants to believe a black family could ever be ordinary. I told someone who wanted me to do this book, that's what it's all about—that you don't have to be Superman or Superwoman to accomplish things. You can be a regular person just like everyone else.

When I talk about normalcy, it was like the Lundquists, our neighbors when we were growing up. They went through the same shenanigans about blessing their family, told their kids to be there at the dinner table, paid attention to their kids, their cleanliness. We were normal that way.

The other thing these writers wanted to do is pigeonhole me as something they wanted me to be—black activist this, feminist that. The truth is, a lot of how I think of myself comes from the farm, a farm gal from Minnesota. One thing you need to know about my background is, it's almost all on the farm. Even people who know me tend to forget that because I've been in the city so long.

The farms in my family's history were for the most part pretty successful, and my relatives that I know about were all free people, no slaves among the relatives that I know of. I know that disappoints the people who think they know all about every black person's history.

My father's father always had land, though I don't know the regulations and conditions. That part of the family, the Allens, they were all born in Missouri. My great-grandfather Allen had five hundred acres, but I don't know how they got land. They farmed lots of corn and therefore had lots of pigs, bacon, and ham. They had some cotton and tobacco.

Some of my mother's people—the Travises—originally came from Rising Sun, Indiana, where my mother was born in the early 1880s. One of my mother's brothers farmed in Rising Sun. They raised corn, and I heard references to cotton. There were certain parts of Indiana with no roads, and they blazed the trail through. It was like when we moved to Pine County in 1913, when I was eight. You have to cut out a lot of brush. The meaning of a trail then was really a road.

The other thing you need to know about my family is that while some people know me as the first black this, the first black that, the truth is, both sides of my family were mixed-race, tremendously mixed. I don't think people always know just how much of that there was in history.

On my father's side, the Allens, it was German and black. My grandfather Allen was black, and my grandmother Allen, she was second-generation German, from the Dresden area, where I'm told they made fine china. There's a smattering of Cherokee—two of my father's brothers even settled in Oklahoma with the Indians. Herbert and Roscoe were the ones that married Indians.

On my mother's side, there had to be a lot of French, Irish, and Seminole. My grandmother's husband came from the Everglades—he was Seminole and black. Those couples, blacks and Indians, mixed all the time. The Irish is where the red streaks in my hair come from—almost all of my brothers and sisters have it, too. One of my sisters, every one of her kids had a band of freckles—that's from grandparents on my mother's side, the Irish influence. I remember once, when I was seventeen and living with my aunt in north Minneapolis, she was washing my hair, and she just turned and yelled to her husband, "Hey Roscoe, she's got all these red streaks"—meaning me. I thought, haven't you ever seen that in a black person before? But she married into the family, and I guess didn't know all the stuff on my mother's side.

As for the French, I do know that Foree was my mother's mother's name. It was originally La Foree somewhere along the line, but they dropped the *La* because it was a burden to most Americans.

I was born Nellie Saunders Allen in 1905, and my name came about because Grandma Foree had been married once before, to a man named Saunders. He was a racehorse breeder named Nelson Saunders. I suppose that might have had something to do with me being so close to horses all my life, I don't know. But I'll tell you all about that when we get to my farm life.

My grandmother Foree was always talking about history. Her background had to be farm, fields of cotton. She died after Mother married Dad in 1904, I think. Because of the Civil War, most all of that generation, most of her people, could read and write, including the black ones. A lot of them, as I get it, associated with the white kids. Only one member of my family didn't read so well—my grandfather on my father's side.

Education was big on both sides of my family, too. My mother was trained as a teacher, which was how she got to Minnesota, and my grandmother Allen on my father's side, well, she was a force when it came to learning. Grandma Allen was born around Dawson, Missouri, near Cape Girardeau, and she became a teacher. She made sure that all her kids went to high school. Out of the eight boys and one girl that she had, all got to the tenth grade. That was higher education at that time, in the mid to late 1800s.

Grandma Allen was quite heavy—it seemed like she ate all the time. She was a big, stern, German woman, and that's another thing that made her such a force.

Now, Grandma Allen said she came out of the very conservative side of German Lutheranism—I think maybe they were Missouri Synod Lutherans. Her husband, my grandfather, was definitely black—a good-looking man from Cape Girardeau, Missouri, a big town in

Mark Twain's books. A lot of Grandfather Allen's people were from around Hannibal, in the tracks of the James brothers. Down there, everyone black and white wasn't allowed to get together—except for blacks to work for whites, or vice versa: whites could work for blacks—which did happen.

My grandfather Allen was also a black Baptist. So it was a pretty natural question: how did they ever get together? Once, when I was a teenager, I asked Grandma Allen point-blank, "How did you get together, the conservative German Lutheran and the Baptist?" I said it just like that.

She said that first, it was those beautiful horses that he rode—that's really how she fell in love. She said, "Oh, those horses, the saddles and the bridles." They were very romantic.

Grandfather Allen was an admirer of horses. There was a group called the Chautauqua, who were entertainers and widespread around the country at that time. They'd go from one small town to the other, like the Barnum and Bailey circuses, but with a serious side. I can see her saying, "Oh, those mustachios." They were the Chautauqua riders, but she was also talking about Grandpa Allen. He had a moustache that came on down—what do you call it?—a handlebar.

I never heard the gory details about Grandpa and Grandma Allen overcoming prejudice in their lives. I heard the families tolerated each other through the church, even though one was Baptist and the other Lutheran.

Someplace along the line, the family that Grandma Allen came out of believed in education for all people. I think the Bible had a lot to do with it. I think she believed the part about us all being God's children. I'll bet you anything she was closer to the Quakers, and that's where a lot of antislavery stuff came from, the Quakers. Grandma Allen had a passion for education, and when I knew her, she just read all the time. What I picked up on there is that you can become bigger than yourself, go beyond your limited experiences, if you read.

She had white skin, and some of her children had very light skin. Uncle Walter, the oldest, he had red hair and freckles, but he was darker. My father, the second child in the family—he was born in 1880—was very light, almost red in the summer. My dad was one of eight boys—the family only had one girl, one sister; I don't know how she survived.

My dad, William Allen, had curls, great big waves in the middle of his head. I thought that was great, so beautiful. When his hair got sweaty, he had these great big ringlets, curls, right in the middle of his head. He grew to be a big man, about six feet, which was certainly big for those times. He loved the physical work, the outdoors.

I do know that a big influence on him educationally, aside from his mother, was growing up listening to speakers from the Freedmen's Bureau, which was big in that part of Missouri where he grew up.

This was part of the antislavery movement that remained after they got rid of slavery, at the religious level, I think. The Freedmen were a group designed to teach the families of former slaves about education and equality, the great values of owning property and raising crops. I think my dad went to every conference they would hold every August. They were in Moberly, Dalton, five or six other country towns in Missouri.

All I know is that Dad said when the Freedmen caravans arrived, the family would load all these kids into the wagon with fried chicken and French bread, and they'd go off to meet. It was like a church get-together, and some of the talk was about freeing each other from slavery's legacy. See, they knew how important history was. Even though they weren't slaves, they knew that the slave mind-set had power in history, and they would have to work hard to overcome it, both to get it out of their own heads and to overcome others who believed it. Today, when people ask me why I am such a demon on knowing the past, I think of how my dad knowing history must have helped him.

When the family talked about this, I was still pretty young, not into organizational things myself yet. But the Freedmen had these agendas—people going into politics, more education, and the right to vote were always on the agenda.

I think it was his mother, Grandma Allen, that pushed him that kind of way, even though she was a white Lutheran. Grandpa, even though he was black, was no factor. He did whatever Grandma told him to do. Dad was there because he worked, and he loved to work. He was as much an entrepreneur as anyone you call that today. I also think it also showed another side of him, the need to reach out to people—just like what I do with my scholarship. Several families that received scholarship money have since contributed to it—people who have been helped helping others. The Freedmen were all about self-help, and that made a big impression. Education again.

With all that in his mind, Dad wanted to leave Dalton to work and own property, and to build up some savings. He went as far as the Montana wheat fields, and he also went to Moose Jaw, Saskatchewan. Wherever there was a barn. He always traveled, but he settled down not too far from the Minnesota River.

What got Dad here was my uncle Walter. Dad was the second oldest to Walter. Walter came to Minneapolis first, then Dad followed him in. Now my dad, he did his little boxcar thing. He was an adventurous, independent man; he literally rode the boxcars from St. Joseph to Minneapolis. Walter, on the other hand, was such a proper gentleman, he'd never think of riding the rails like my dad. Walter was quite a churchman—I think he came here by following a minister up here. He had a job with the linseed oil mills.

They were a little church family, and Walter gave Dad a room to bunk in. He came here just in time for a Minnesota winter, after helping with the harvest in Saskatchewan. Dad did some work at Walter's workplace, the linseed oil company, and he also worked at a gun club. That was a private gun club on the Minnesota River in Lakeville, and he made some money helping out the shooting men. But he made quite a bit more on the side, trapping on the river in Lakeville. I don't know if his bosses knew that trapping became a side income for him, but he bought horses and a wagon with the money. Like I said, he was quite an entrepreneur.

My mother, Gladys Foree, grew up in Carrollton, Kentucky. I don't know how my mom came to read so readily, because I couldn't tell there was anyone quite like Grandma Allen in her family. Most of that encouragement, I think, was done through the churches. Even the white women there taught black kids to read and write, not just in Indiana, but Kentucky, too. My grandmother Allen said that was also true in Missouri. A lot of good things came from the churches.

Mom ended up going to a teachers college in Louisville, Kentucky—Louisville Teachers Normal. All the teachers colleges were called "normals" back then. It wasn't hard for Mother to go to college, because the money was there—from racehorses!

Remember Nelson Saunders, the man I was named after? He was a horse trainer, a breeder. A lot of people who owned horses, if they found a black person who knew horses, they would turn theirs over to him immediately. This came from slavery days, the feeling of security white people had when blacks worked the stables.

My mother told me that my uncle Nelson served more than one family's horses. He also raced, although he drove a sulky, for harness racing. His money allowed her to go to school, that was basically it!

She graduated in 1902. It was quite rare for a black woman to graduate, but apparently everybody at this Louisville Normal Teachers College was of some kind of freedom or equal opportunity persuasion, even though the majority had to be white women. One of their regular speakers was Ida B. Wells, kind of a hefty black women who made the rounds for the [antilynching movement]. When you put those things together philosophically, people at that school had to be thinking about the equality of all races. Otherwise, the likes of Ida B. Wells would never get a chance to speak.

My mom came to Minnesota by way of New York and Chicago—she had two aunts in Chicago who ran a great big old boardinghouse. Mom stayed with them, filled in as a teacher on the south side of Chicago, teaching mostly Mexican kids. That's what the black teachers did. Even though she couldn't speak the language, she worked out some way to communicate with them.

She came here to get a job teaching in Minneapolis. She never told me exactly why she came, but I think it was those two aunts. A lot of people passed through the boardinghouse, and some of 'em had to be going to Minneapolis-St. Paul. She heard it was a good place to be a teacher, and she wanted her kids to be schooled in such a place, even though she wasn't even married then.

After arriving, both my parents made their way to Bethesda Church, Eleventh Avenue South and Eighth Street in Minneapolis. They were both pretty good singers, and they volunteered for the choir.

Here's something else they had in common: they both came out of pretty religious families, but they were also independent thinkers, which allowed them to question the justness of God—how would God allow enslavement? A just God wouldn't allow it. My mother was a Baptist, she sang in the choir. My dad was a Lutheran, but it didn't take him long to become a Baptist—women are strong influences, and his father had been a Baptist before my grandmother Allen married him.

They knew each other a long time—two years—but not by today's standards. When Dad met Mom, he was not quite a farmer yet. He already had a house and a team of horses. Dad married my mother at Bethesda in 1904, then they got the first farm in Lakeville, Minnesota, just south of the Twin Cities. Their honeymoon was driving from Minneapolis to Lakeville, about twenty-five miles. They moved to this house a stone's throw from what became our first farm.

He met the owner of the house when he was sashaying to the gun club, and rented the place. Their house was pretty ancient. There was development out there even then. The west eighty acres was always developed to Orchard Lake. There were wheat fields, diary farms. It was very fertile land, and we had a pretty view of it. That's where I was born.

Chapter 2

Siblings

I'm the oldest, born December 17, 1905. If you didn't know that I'm the oldest, you'd probably guess from how headstrong I am. My memory has always been very good—I can remember my mother and father when I was about three years old, and I remember my first incident when I was about three and a half. How do I know what that first memory was? I checked with my mother.

This will tell you something about my personality. The farm I was born at in Lakeville, we called it the Toltz place, because Toltz owned the land; he was a St. Paul lawyer. We raised corn and potatoes, and also some oats.

Anyway, we had a man who lived at the farm. He was very fat and wasn't well; he had dropsy or some bloated disease. Someone asked if he could stay out on our farm and do a little work and get a little pay. We had a little wood walkway out to the road, with wood slats that kind of went diagonal. This old man liked to put a chair against a picket fence and stretch his legs across the walk. I was moving out the kitchen, to the road, and he was in my way. I was so indignant about that—people always said be nice to old people, but I remember very clearly fussing with him, telling him to get out of my way. Remember, I was three. I called myself Nay then, and my mother said I put my hands on my hips and said, "Get out of Nay's way!" I certainly remember him being in my way. He said he would not get out of my way, that I needed to get out of his way. Now, this man had planted tomato seeds, and I went around back and got one of the stobs—a tool, not sharp, for digging holes to put the plant in—and came back and started sticking him in the ribs. He called for Mother to help him, so I must have hurt him despite me being three years old and all the fat on him!

I ended up with eight brothers and sisters, and we got along pretty good. We all grew up on farms, and we had some problems when we got into the inheritance of land, but we worked it out.

Richard is the next oldest to me, fourteen months younger. Even though a lot of first kids can be selfish, I got along pretty well with him—we did have flare-ups, but not many. He was a horseman—he loved the horses. If there's such a thing as liking horses more than me, he was it.

When we went to school, I was always in a fight because big boys would take after Richard. I was a big, rangy kid—you would call me a tomboy today. The first boy I beat, I almost scratched him to death. My father had to take this boy to the doctor and get his face stitched up. The undercurrent might have been that Richard was black, even though no one said so and I didn't think of it at the time. I was eight. I think the next fight I got into was when I was twelve; I knocked this boy down and got right in his face. He was fourteen, but I might have had more muscles.

I never fought girls—I might have pulled their hair, but it was always boys who got in my way. I'd wiggle around them and got some blows into their face and head.

Richard was a little slighter than most boys, and he was slow—just could not do things very fast. I would read books in no time, but he'd bumble around and read every word and ponder it. He did that with car manuals—he'd read every word, ponder them, before he did something. He was very deliberate and very good with the cattle; if something had to be administered to them, you can bet your bottom dollar that every thread of a bandage would be in place.

That's why it was so ironic how he died. He was a farmer, and he got killed in a tractor accident at forty-seven. Everybody liked him because he was so exact. After my father died, Richard farmed our farm in Hinckley. He was doing some maintenance on the county road, and the tractor turned over—the shoulders where he was tending were built up quite high. I still feel he went to sleep coming out of the driveway to do the mowing. This was 1952 or 1953.

And then there was another sister, Mayme, three years younger. She died of diabetes. Then there was Herbert, who was five years younger. He and I got along real well. He was six-three, six-four, a very strong person—my father said he didn't know his own strength. He was quite fast and had the strength and stamina to keep going. We were pretty much alike. You see me jumping around, well, he had ten times as much energy, *zoom, zoom, zoom!*

He liked history. He knew the dates of all the presidents, for example. He was the next one to me in milking, because Richard did the horses. He became a farmer. He farmed with Richard, and they bought another farm a mile from the home farm. They helped the old man after Mother died and I left.

Herbert, he had kind of an accident, too, and it affected him terribly. He was splitting logs, and he sat on the log splitter. He sat on this green log instead of standing over it, and the machine split it too easily and the wedge got his whole privates. It took all the fight out of him. My father was not too far away when this happened. Herbert was in his early thirties when it happened, and he died at thirty-two.

Then there was Gladys. She died a year ago. She was eight years younger. First thing about her is that she had nine children, so she was pretty busy being a mother. Early in her life she worked in a restaurant and lived on Girard Avenue North in Minneapolis. Her husband was a leader on the railroad, Bill Patterson.

On the farm, I thought she was lazy as hell when it came to milking or washing dishes. I'd be in the house washing dishes, and Herbert liked to tease me. He'd say, "Oh you're washing dishes . . . where's Gladys?" Gladys could be mean as hell when she wanted to be. We got along better after she had all of her kids and we both got older. She did a great job taking care of her kids—and this family was poor. For a while there, it looked like I had a niece or nephew graduating from North High every year. I bought a lot of food for them.

My next brother is Cortland. He's still living, in Ohio, and he's ten years younger. He's very fiery, always on the go. Cortland was a man at eleven. He liked all kinds of machinery, whereas Richard didn't learn to drive until he was twenty-two.

I remember one year after I left for Minneapolis. I came home on a vacation, and he came running in the house and said come on out and help me! I said, what do you want me to do, and he said, put out a fire! Sure enough, out by the gashouse, the ground was on fire. He was eleven years old, and I reprimanded him. I said, you can't put water on that fire, you have to spade it. He had spilled like fifty-five gallons of gas trying to get it in some machine. He said, what are you punishing me for, don't you know when a man gets to be eleven years old, he knows everything? I said, yes, I see the fire!

Cortland ran a business, a garage, for forty years. He was all set to go over and kill Hitler, but he wound up the property of General Motors. Anyone who was kind of good at a skill, they shipped out to businesses. He was shipped to Detroit and trained about eighty men. He did a good thing when he went there. He wasn't deep into civil and human rights, but he had forty workers, black and white. He was the boss, and a mixed crew got him used to working for all rights. He could take anything and put it together to make a car out of it.

How Cortland got to Youngstown, Ohio, has to do with my next brother, Clemmet, named after one of my father's brothers. Clem was eleven years younger than me and was killed at twelve or thirteen. He and Cortland were always together, and Clemmy would do anything for Cortland. They got to monkeying around with old cars—put together a Dodge chassis and Chevy engine, for example, and they could just fly with cars like that. He was a damn good driver, but not to the satisfaction of Mrs. Jones, one of our neighbors, who would complain about his driving.

One day, a car he was in with no top flipped over, and he was killed. That day, Cortland was the driver. I don't think Cortland has ever gotten over it. We still get to talking about the family, and he gets so quiet—usually he's very talkative. We went up and visited the family graveyard a couple of weeks ago, and I noticed he was very quiet. After my mom died, Cortland didn't stay around long; he was fourteen or fifteen, and he came down to the city and stayed with me. Then he took off one day, and I got a call—he was in Youngstown, Ohio.

Almeda came after Clem. She was thirteen years younger, I washed her diapers. She was good, lives in New Hope now. She has three boys. Later in her life, she got mixed up with liquor, and the family told her she had to sell this house she had north and get herself an apartment. The culture around where she was just wasn't very good. She belonged to the same union I was in. She worked as executive housekeeper at the old Radisson on Seventh.

Both of my sisters were much lighter than me. We all had that mixture of red hair, one way or the other. Both of their hair was really considered to be auburn. It wasn't flaming red, but neither was it dark. I guess around certain people, I'm light, but I considered myself to be dark because of those girls. My hair was definitely brown, even with the red streak.

My sisters, they *never* tried to pass. My family was crazy about that. Even with my grandnephews, the one at River Falls, he's very light, but he joined the black caucus, and when you see him with all those blacker people, it looks strange. But I thought, great. In an overall diverse cultural setting, his intelligence ranks right up there, and philosophically he's black, even though his mother is white, an Olson even! His name is Kyle Olson Patterson.

I've had that happen, passing. When I was younger, I was much lighter, as most people are, especially people of Native American and black persuasion. I have a picture taken in 1950—the whole executive board of my union—and my complexion doesn't look any darker than these Yugoslav people, like George Naumoff and Tony Mancheff. Up in Hinckley, we had two neighbors about a mile or two from us. One was Bieloff and the other was Toloff. A lot of stuff you hear about the war from Yugoslavia today, my gosh, it's shades of George Naumoff. He would always refer to himself as Croat, not a Yugoslav.

This aunt of mine who was married to my uncle Roscoe, on my

father's side, she was a Chippewa—Roscoe actually was married to two of 'em, one from Oklahoma, another from Winona. His wife Myrtle and I had identical complexions. When I was younger, a little heavier, people thought we were both black in black communities, and in Native American communities, that we were both Native Americans. Roscoe was my father's youngest brother, and he was only six years older than me.

It was a political thing, not trying to pass. We realized that discrimination was going on, we all read quite a bit. We developed a blackness philosophy that was not characteristic of everyone in the black community. We'd do something with politics and work and definitely not camouflage it. It probably would have been easy to camouflage for some of the family, but there was no strength to that. I just liked the comfort of being what I'm supposed to be and what I am. There's a lot of comfort and security in just being who you are. You might think trying to be white is safer, but I had seen the other side. I knew women who had gone to work in department stores, who were quite white, and when certain people found out they weren't, they got quite shaken up. These women sometimes lost their jobs.

My last sister was Dorothy, who was born with a kidney problem and lived only six months. She had to go to the doctor every day. She had some rash, like eczema, all over her body, and the doctor said that's the poison, the urine poison. She was the youngest. My mom was forty-seven when she had Dorothy.

There was nothing Mom could do about kids because there was no Planned Parenthood. Most women dried up before forty-seven, but Grandma Allen didn't hit menopause until her fifties! I was scared to death it would happen to me, but I went to Dr. David Eisenstadt, and told him, "You've known my sisters since knee-high to whatever, is there anything women can take to get through menopause?" He said, "Liver and hormones," and gave me half a hormone shot. I think it did work, because the minute I turned fifty I didn't suffer through menopause, no flash or anything, I just dried up. I turned fifty and it was all over.

Chapter 3

The Farms

In Nellie's early life, she lived in two counties. Dakota County, south of Minneapolis, contains Lakeville and rolling hillsides, where Nellie's family owned their first two farms between 1905 and 1918. Sometimes, events placed in "Dakota County" refer to things that happened on both the Toltz and the Tobacky farm. Pine County, one hundred miles north and a bit east, contains slightly poorer but still good soils. Nellie spent her teen years there before coming to the Twin Cities. The closest village to the Pine County farm is Clover Township, and Hinckley is the closest big town.

The Toltz place, where the first five of us were born, was right up to Buck Hill, the place where everybody skis now. When we moved to our second house, which we called the Tobacky place after its owner, we actually pastured Buck Hill, even though we lived farther away from it. Pasturing was only in the summer months, when the grass was growing, and here's how it worked. Dad got the male population of cows, which were castrated. You'd run 'em on that grass on the hill, then bring them in in October, and feed 'em hard corn. You'd get steers at the trough who would feed all day. They were beef cows—you'd just put the fat and weight on 'em. It was blue-ribbon meat—when they're young enough, the meat's not tough. When it came to beef we ate eighteen-month-old livestock. We wouldn't kill anything under eighteen months. If it's a lot younger, it's known as veal.

Toltz was two eighty-acre pieces, but it was all one farm. One was for the house and farm, and the part ran all the way to Orchard Lake. I think it crossed someone else's forty. Somebody probably sold the owner a bill of goods, since he was a professional man in St. Paul who maybe didn't know any better. Maybe he couldn't do any better. The house there wasn't very large, two rooms upstairs, and a living room and kitchen downstairs. My dad put on my summer kitchen. I liked that room a lot. It was a lean-to on one side of the house, without all of the chimneys for the heavy stove like in the main kitchen. The insulation was thinner. You had it there for summer, the cooking stove, to keep it from heating up the rest of the house. A lot of people had summer kitchens then. There was a lot of breeze that ran through it, and you could see the summer stars.

With five kids and two bedrooms, well, now you know why we needed to move. The people that owned that Tobacky place, they owned the hardware store. He wanted to rent that land out to whatever farmer would rent it, because he wanted to run the hardware store, and his kids were too young to farm. It was a hundred-and-sixty-acre farm, altogether. I don't think my dad ran into any problems renting it because he was black. Mr. Tobacky just didn't want to farm it himself.

The Tobacky place was a large place, well finished with lots of hardwood. There was a big room off of the dining room, and the dining room opened up into a big kitchen. This big room was about twelve to fourteen feet long; we used it as a bedroom, usually when someone had been taken ill. We gave Grandma and Grandpa Allen that room when they moved up here in 1914. They could use the kerosene stove. Upstairs, that house had three bedrooms, two big ones. Over the dining room, there was a big bedroom—it was always the warmest part of the house during the coldest part of the winter. We would run drum heaters in the bedrooms—like another little stove, with pipes at the top and bottom, one to a floor. It was so warm and toasty. It was maybe twelve by fourteen and held my parents in a double bed. Then the drum came up between another big bed with two of us in two doubles—look—two girls in one and two boys in the other. We wound up facing each other, my parents on one side and the kids on the other.

We talked to each other, pinched each other. I remember making my sister Gladys so mad when I took a handful of crackers to bed. After dinner, I'd still feel like something to eat. I was the oldest, and there was eight years' difference with the next-oldest sister, Gladys. She didn't like to do any kind of work around the house. My brother and I would laugh about it. You'd always find her in the barn or the haystack—she'd say she was just resting.

The family moved for more cows, more milk, as much as more house. We didn't have the area in the barn for cows at the Toltz place. There was a large area at Tobacky's for horses, all stone and concrete where the barn was, and we milked thirty cows. It seemed like we had more cows, fifty, when we moved to Hinckley. The dream was to keep all those kids working, so you had to have lots of cows. There was kind of a joke among farmers that had families—just as soon as one of your kids got old enough to milk, the old man went to town and bought ten more cows! That was not entirely true with our old man—he was enough of an entrepreneur that he didn't wait for us kids. He'd contract with people to take a few cows, so he could add ten without us.

This morning when I woke up, I started to think about milking cows. I started milking when I was six years old. Kids at that age started working in those days. One cow—her name was Spot. I knew just where she stood in barn, I remember that vividly. She was either Gurnsey or Hereford, they both had spots. She lived for fifteen years and died a natural death. I kind of liked to milk—I remember I would lay up against her and get warm when the weather was cold.

The cows and horses were all in one barn at Tobacky's, but there was a partition. Just as you came in the door, there were somewhere between fifteen and twenty-five cows, with a division for hay on the other side. We were the milking machine—especially me, not even my dad milked as many. The barn smelled like cows and horses. The one in Lakeville had a division with the cows in the subbasement, the rock foundation, and horses upstairs. The main level for each was different,

different doors. That's where I kept my skates. The skates were on the cow level, which is where the lake was.

Both of the farms in Lakeville had lakes on 'em. I learned to skate at the Toltz place, and when we moved to the other place, I was handling horses quite fluently, which had something to do with skating. I hitched up this horse, put it on the big scoop shovel that we usually used to grade roads, and I cleaned this lake, so I had my own little skating area! You can bet I kept that scoop clean, and had a pair of skates in the barn. If I had fifteen minutes, I would do it. I loved to skate, especially at the Tobacky place.

When I was just coming into the equation in 1911 with my one cow, we had two hired hands then. Dad eventually doubled the herd, so we had fifty cows during the depression. I milked straight through until I left for the city at seventeen. Probably when I was twelve or thirteen, I was milking thirty cows a day—fifteen in the morning and fifteen at night. Let me tell you, my arms and legs were strong!

I started riding a horse about the same age as I started milking, six. Dad threw me up on the back of a horse—a big one. It wasn't like those Clydesdales you see on the Budweiser commercial—it was a lighter horse, but still a heavy worker. There was actually a team—Barney and George. I remember going up and down the tallest one, Barney. Oh, I liked that! I rode on a western saddle, but by the time I was twelve or thirteen years old, I'd just jump up on him bareback!

I always felt close to horses. I use to just lean up against them. Did you know that when you do that, if a horse wrinkles his nose, he likes you? Horses would wrinkle their noses and put them up against me. I'd greet them.

When I was quite small, my dad ran horses with just the halter on. I would jump on and ride on their backs, with no saddle and no bridle. You can guide the horse with just your hands, on either side of their neck. We did have saddles—great big leather ones. We had a rider's, or racer's, saddle. It had a hole in the middle, but I didn't like it, it was hard. Plus, my common sense said a saddle like that helped the horse's back to breathe, so why not uncover him as much as possible?

I remember one time I just jumped on a horse and rode to the house. The horse's name was Bobby—I just loved to ride him everywhere. He'd do whatever I wanted him to; I knew him almost like he was a human being. We went down by the creek, and then up the lane to the house—I must have ridden that horse two miles. My mother was in the kitchen, and we had a great big kitchen with low windows. She saw me ride by. When I came in the door, she had the cornstarch ready! She said, let me powder you. The lower part of my leg was fat— I had very large muscles. My mother was a very observant lady—she said, you would ride horses bareback at fifty miles an hour! When I was a kid and I got sick, my mother always had spirits of peppermint in the closet and we got well right away! It's still a good thing to do!

I remember we also used baking soda, back when people hardly knew what that meant beyond cooking. We used it to sanitize things. In 1914-15, we just started using Colgate toothpaste. There had been several days before anyone went to town, and my mom said we've got to use baking soda, but we all thought it was terrible. Not too many years later, though, I used baking soda regularly!

We did use the pharmacy quite a bit—but the stuff we used on animals was often good for human beings. Certain liniments we used on horses we used on ourselves, too, for joints and muscles.

We had the flu the year we moved to Hinckley. The two people who didn't get it were myself and my father. My father was doing all the milking, and I was doing all the cooking, so it worked out. That was a bad year for the flu, because it killed off so many people, in 1918. I didn't see any people die. I did see people die from diphtheria and scarlet fever. I think the cleanliness helped us a little.

There was quite a cholera epidemic among pigs at that time, but we were lucky. My dad had lots of medicine and lots of veterinarians, and we kept our pig barn so clean. Sprayed the pigs, too, with whatever kind of medicine.

When I was seven years old, I went to the hay field with my dad—my brother Richard wasn't old enough yet to drive the team. My dad harnessed up George to the hay mower; day after day we spent in the fields. I never wore a dress—it was coveralls and rubber-soled boy's shoes. I was instinctively geared to what boys would do.

Some of my first enlightenment came in an argument with my brother Richard. We needed someone to carry in the wood—Richard was a bit lazy, too, and I'd been mowing hay all day. I told Richard he hadn't done anything all day, and that carrying in the wood was boy's work. My old man said, "There's no such thing as boy's work in this family." He gave me a hard look and said, "Let me tell you something, young lady—there's nothing you can't do if you make up your mind to do it." I never forgot what Dad said, and I've been trying to live up to it ever since.

We were fearless, mostly. I remember me and my brother Herbert used to take dynamite and blow a hole in the creek, so it got like eleven feet deep. I liked to trap and hunt. When I was eight years old, I had my first twenty-two. I was a pretty good mechanic. I was a mechanic on a Model T, and who couldn't be on that car? It was so simple—all you had to do was screw a nut on a bolt.

I remember asking my mom many years later after I grew up, how much of this was the rights of women and how much was it to get work out of me? I remember my grandma, who was listening, just raised her eyebrow, which to me meant I was reading it right.

I learned a lot of things about men just hanging around our kitchen table in Dakota County. Certainly some of the men were bad. There was one of our neighbors who lived up the hill, he beat his wife, but he wouldn't scar her up too much. I knew because I would hear my mom talk about how Mrs. Streefland was doing and whoever she was talking with would say, "Oh, John beat her up last night." This woman, John's wife, and their son did all the milking. And she would come over after the milking, her and her older son, looking for sympathy. Now, if I got *too* close to the table, mother would beckon me to go outside.

I think the way we settled on it was that Dad said any man that would hit a woman was a coward. I knew that a coward was bad. I think a lot of his talk was meant for my brother. It was not that early in life for Dad. The traditional thing was for a woman to get beaten up if the man thought she acted up. Remember, this was before women even had the right to vote!

The other day was the seventh of May, and I was thinking about this because it was my father's birthday. In Lakeville, Dad had three or four teams of horses in the field, and he gave Grandpa one team to farm. My uncle Roscoe also had teams in the field with us. If I remember right, one of the hired men was there. What was so important, what made me think about it, was that it was snowing—great big flakes of snow. I said it shouldn't be snowing on May seventh, and Mom said it can snow whenever God wants it to!

We were always the first to have stuff. Like the Model T Ford. Our neighbors, the Streeflands had one, and then a man in Lakeville named Charlie Sauser became a Ford salesman. Charlie was not just a car salesman, he was the barber in town, too. My dad went to him to get what he called a "city shave." I guess, Charlie, being the salesman that he was, came to the house to do the finishing, and next thing, Dad woke up the next morning with a car. We were either the first or the second people to have things. Dad worked morning, noon, and night, and had money to do those things, plus he was forward-looking, forward-reaching about what would save time and improve the conditions for the family.

We went to the Bethesda Church. I loved Sunday school—we had a good Sunday school—and my parents would go to church, too. Despite my mother singing in that Baptist choir, we weren't that religious. I like the Bible for the historicalness of it but not so much the religion, which I got from my father. He was talking about the bondage of black people, slaves—what we were reading in the black press about the atrocities at that time, the lynchings. He said, "You have to believe God is just," but he didn't believe it himself. He put the question that way—you know, if there was a just God, this wouldn't happen.

My mom actually quit going to church long before my dad did. I never realized then quite why—she had to cook Sunday dinner, and finish up ironing while we were in Sunday school. I was seven, eight, nine.

I remember Reverend Moody from Lakeville, he came from a different church to talk the Bible with us. It was a Union Sunday school, which means they took kids from all kinds of Christian religions. He was a Presbyterian, and he would just ride the circuit kind of. There were even a few Catholics who came to Sunday school. I never argued the point too much. Took for granted what they told me.

It was mainly social, going to church and Sunday school. The New Testament, I do like that. I would like to have been in the position of Jesus Christ, to do the community work as he did, to get around, talk to people—though I might've drawn the line at being nailed to the cross. There was one big page out of David and Goliath in our illustrated Bible. I kind of believed in that story. See, it was about war, and I figured they have to tell the truth with that. I was kind of in a childish mind, I guess—if they're killing up on people, they had better tell the truth.

I'm still not religious, unless you call politics religion. It's what you believe in strongly, isn't it? You could almost call my politics my religion, my God. I believe in the good and bad of people. I can't say I'm a disbeliever of all things religious, either. I guess I'm a pretty practical person. You talk about spirits, well, I'll tell you there's something wiggling around in my apartment. I don't know if I believe in ghosts, but I believe in that. This could be a ghost—it's handy, comfortable. I think religion serves that purpose for a lot of people.

Lakeville had a strong Irish community. Irish people were radical from the time they first set foot in this country. They came from the potato famine, when that set in. Mother knew all the Irish songs, *Danny Boy* and all of that.

One thing I liked about the community of Lakeville was the thread of decency. The religious belief just didn't kill it off—and you know, sometimes different religions, like the Catholics and the Protestants, fight so much they murder everything they say they believe in! Politics and class also played a role. The community at that time was really middle-class people, born into that. Everybody had enough to eat, a church, and a team of horses. We also had some poor—mostly the people who worked for everybody else—but nearly everyone had eighty acres. You didn't have to complain too much.

I think education had a whole lot to do with everybody getting along, too. Education was everything to everyone there. The German Lutherans, the Holland Lutherans, the Irish Catholics, we all wanted the same thing. All of us expressed our desire to go to the university. Dad had a different idea for me—he was acquainted with Carleton College, and sending me there was kind of a dream. When the time came we just couldn't afford it—it's like what happens with a lot of great dreams, it doesn't always materialize. I didn't make it, but one of my grandnieces did.

To a great extent, if you were a decent family, you were decent enough to stand toe-to-toe with anybody in Dakota County. In Dakota County I went to school with everything! We had upper-class people who had year-round homes at Orchard Lake and Crystal Lake, and we had people with lice on their heads—that drove Mom crazy. My feeling is that I learned so much from them and they learned from me.

I think I enjoyed mostly the culture, the diverse differences. Of course, we had no name for it then. I guess we called it nationality. Mostly it came back to cooking or sewing. There was still a bit of dressing and eating from the old country. I remember Streefland, he went back to Holland, and brought me back a maroon dress. I remember it well—the brass buttons came down on both sides, there was so much decoration, the curlicues.

They maybe learned the same thing from me—they loved my mother's cooking. Regardless of nationality, they got to know Mother's cooking—the cakes and cookies especially. She cut those cookies large—I don't know if she used a can that was bigger.

I have a memory of my folks talking about how bad it was, racism, though they said not so much around them. We always subscribed to the *Chicago Defender* [a black paper]—it was as readily in our house as the *Minneapolis Morning Tribune*. We got the *Chicago Defender*—I don't remember anything specific as far as incidents go, everything was kind of general. There was an awareness of racism in your own life. The awareness was to watch out for certain people.

I did hear about outright anti-Semitism, though. I heard my uncle Roscoe, who was living with us at the time, say something to my mother in the kitchen, something about the ignorance of other people calling people names. Roscoe said some neighbor called the Straniks, our neighbors, Christ killers. Of course, they were Jewish.

Pine County was a little different place to be black. We were renting in Lakeville, but we bought in Pine County, which is why we moved up there. We moved because after World War I, all the doughboys came back and wanted their old jobs—and lots of them were farmers. Everybody and his brother tried to gouge soldiers. They wanted to work, so land prices shot up.

There was some property in Lakeville on the market. The old man had been looking in the market for sometime, but land was just too expensive, running around a thousand dollars an acre. For dairy land, that was just too much money, so Dad decided to cash out his holdings and go to Pine County, which was farther north, up by Hinckley.

The land wasn't as good, but it was cheap and we could buy a lot of it. Herman Streese, he was a neighbor in Lakeville, owned the land in Pine County. I remember my mother wasn't feeling good about it, but my dad said, "I'm going to buy it on the spot." That's what rising land prices made you do. We moved to Hinckley in March 1918. When we got there, it turned out we were so far above most people in Pine County in terms of education and holdings it wasn't even funny. We had an automobile, and fifty cows pretty soon; Dad was a hard worker and very successful.

Our house in Pine County was beautiful—it started out as a hunting lodge. It had four bedrooms, and my dad built on an extra kitchen, fourteen by twenty-four—my mom kind of liked that. It didn't take too long to get the idea from poorer people living there that we were kind of snooty.

But our skin color was the big reason we were not too desired when we first came to Pine County. We did hear rumors that, before we got there, someone was trying to circulate a petition to prevent us from living there. But one person who had a lot of land up there, John Streefland, went to bat for us. He told folks up there, "This man Allen, he's worked hard, has a good herd, and is going to need hired men. Why, he may be responsible for four or five jobs, working on the farm." He said, "You folks are going to bite off your nose despite your face!"

I would have loved to have seen their faces when Streefland told them that—they're black but they've got money! And we did hire four or five men, Mahoneys and Dawsons.

I remember there was a woman, a township assessor, who was so afraid to be alone that she asked me to ride with her every Saturday morning. She was riding to take the account of everybody's holdings to be properly assessed for taxes. She rode her horse and I rode my horse. I didn't know that she was a racist originally. She was one of the people who carried the gossip that the Becks were racists, and that made me think she was, too. She came off like she loved people, but there was an undercurrent that she didn't. She never said anything exactly that showed her feelings, but when she was telling us about the Becks, she seemed racist. I don't know if it was the tone of her voice, or what.

She started working her route in the dark; as a woman, she was lucky to have the job, and she bent over backwards to keep it. Had she mentioned that she was afraid to Dad, well, he and his good friend Ben Irons were on the township board, and the board might have said, "Well, you're a woman, you don't need the job." She knew I was good with horses and could beat up on most of the boys. Why did I go with her if she was racist? I guess I thought she was just ignorant, and if I rode with her maybe she might get it.

The first time I ever got the sense that I personally was different was when this boy, Orville, called my sister a nigger, and I beat him up. I didn't hesitate at all to take on a boy. He was a little younger than me, I was thirteen or fourteen and he was twelve. I'd heard this happening to people, but he just blurted it out. I would listen to my folks, so I thought he must be listening to his folks, that's where he got it from.

I remember that hearing that word was a big shock. Gladys didn't pay much attention when she got called that name, but I did. My folks never let us use that phrase; it was not familiar, and I didn't know the rancor until I heard it from someone else. I pulled this boy over to the well platform at school, got him on something hard and beat his head in. I don't know if it made me more wary after that, but I read stuff in the *Chicago Defender* about this, and I took it more personally after that.

I remember these wealthy people, the Beck family, who had a good John Deere tractor—and no one knew how to run it! The older Beck told my father that they couldn't operate the tractor, and my father said his younger brother, Roscoe, could run it. They hired Roscoe to run it and train one of their sons to run it. They couldn't even get it out in the field. That always seemed like a conundrum to me—how could they be racist toward us and need our brains?!

Most of my work on the farm, from the time I started with Spot, was milking, every year, more cows, more cows. I had some other jobs in the summer—I weeded the potato field in Dakota County, and the rutabagas in Pine County. They were a specialty up there—turnips and rutabagas. A little bit lighter soil there.

I did plowing and cultivating. There is a process during a planting called blind cultivating—my father would wait for me to do the blind cultivation of corn. It's already planted, and the imprint in the soil is still there. You cultivate to a point so that you are guided by the first wheel track, and throw in dirt into the wheel track, which is your marker, the wheel print of the seeder. The seeder has made a little indentation, and you make a mound clear across the field. Looks like a mound where the seed is.

There's two kinds of corn, what is called the drilled corn and the check corn. I would plow the check corn, which is the Cadillac of corn, what you fatten animals on for food. In Dakota, the production of corn wasn't too much, but up in Pine County, three-quarters of the field was drill corn. The drill corn lets the planter plant one seed after another. The check corn is a check-off system, a wire that would trip two to three kernels into the ground. The drill corn was silage corn—which was so important to farms in Pine County, because we were dairy people. We had two big silos of it.

In Dakota County we grew wheat, potatoes, corn on three hundred-some acres. We had milk cows and lots of horses—all of the land at that time, or ninety percent of it, was plowed by horses. There were lots of pigs at both places. We had chickens, though that was pretty much a smaller operation. My mother had an even smaller operation than that, with turkeys—it was her holiday business. I guess that's where pin money comes from—the turkey's pin feathers. Mothers around there referred to their flocks as pin money. Many seemed to raise little flocks for holiday butchering. That was a part of the culture at that time.

In Pine County we grew pretty much the same things, but Mom did not raise turkeys up there—it was a rougher climate, too cold. There were heavier rains; people may not realize it, but a hundred miles north makes a big difference. The farm there was fifty percent livestock. My father was thinking in terms of dairying every day of his life. We took twenty-five cows from Dakota County to Pine, and we weren't there very long before we doubled the herd.

You can bet I've cut and peeled and skinned a lot of wood. My dad was into the supplemental business of pulp wood, which made paper. We cut it down to the right length and peeled the bark—you got a dollar to a dollar-fifty more per stick if it was peeled before it was shipped to the pulp mills. I used to strip the bark for ten cents apiece from these big logs eight, nine, ten feet long.

We had two dogs, one we moved from Dakota County, which was Rover—he ran with wolves and coyotes. The other one was Mike. They were both collie extractions. They would help round up cows and horses. My father believed in running horses in the pasture. If there was good green grass, there were horses in the pasture.

In Pine County, we shipped stuff like rutabagas and potatoes from a railroad terminal at Askov, Minnesota, northeast from Hinckley. We always had enough to have fresh vegetables in the basement year-round—potatoes, rutabagas, cabbage, and Hubbard squash year-round. They just kept in the cool basement.

During the depression the farm took care of our family. We ate beans and potatoes, and the milk—we had a lot of calcium. We used to joke sometimes that the cows, who didn't always eat that well when times were rough, gave skim, not whole milk! A lot of families were not getting enough milk—we gave five families separated milk every morning, which we had fed to the pigs, chickens, and dogs. We took just enough to give to the people! I don't know if anyone who drank it was one of the people who didn't want us moving there because we had black skin.

Chapter 4

Dad

I remember once, one of my brothers, Herbert, said after my first marriage, "I know why you and Clyde"—my husband at the time—"didn't get along." Herbert said, "You knew every Goddamn thing under the sun, and so did he. You're just like the old man!"

Herbert knew I was a chip off the old man in attitude and makeup. My dad was very sure of himself, very confident. He was the apple of his mother's eye, and he was very intelligent—a natural intelligence, he read everything. He worked hard and he wouldn't let anyone cheat him. He grew up never doubting he was as good as everyone else, and he was stubborn.

I think one of the things Herbert was picking up on was that while he respected the old man, I kind of worshiped him. Not that we didn't disagree—we were both stubborn.

I do know that my platform is the same as my father's: equal opportunity, good education, and good health. Under equal opportunity, you've got a quality education. With good health and a job, what else is there? Love? Oh, by all means, yes—but I'm ninety-four now, remember.

A criticism close friends have of me is that I don't think of myself enough. But what has made me tick is what's best for humanity. A lot of it is triggered by what my parents thought of me. My dad thought very highly of me. I felt pretty proud of that, the confidence he had in me, and I want to live up to that.

Politically, Dad did not come out of the Democrat Party—if anything, his family had been Republican radicals. And not like the radicals they have today! The Republicans were the party of Lincoln once, you know. They believed in the rights of all people, and they fought slavery to the death.

My grandmother Allen, a white woman and a privileged person, she remembers when Yankee soldiers came around to confiscate their furnishings, even some of their land, in Dalton, Missouri. That's the reason so many of our family turned up in Keokuk, Iowa. They were escaping to Yankee territory so they wouldn't loot our land.

The rest of our family never talked about slaves. That was one of the things that befuddled me when I was older. Just about every black I met later could trace themselves back to slaves, but I couldn't. Maybe they didn't talk about slavery because they didn't want to be in the slave mind—though some other black people talked about it like a badge of distinction! It could have been a number of things—maybe they grew up distrusting being public about it. A lot of people lost land, the black side did not have control of property like they should have. On the theory of forty acres and a mule for freed slaves after the Civil War, a lot of land was designated for blacks, but a lot of white officers in the county, they used courts to confiscate acreage. Maybe my family didn't want to remember losing their property—they knew the trickery of the whites.

I heard a little bit about white trickery with other families. I think it was simple greed and opportunity. But my father's folks, they were from Missouri, and that was the state of the Missouri Compromise. My father always talked about the Dred Scott case—he was a slave from Missouri who came to live at Fort Snelling in Minnesota. That case was where the Supreme Court said black people weren't total human beings, they were chattel slaves who were owned body and soul. Dad always said a lot of the attitude of white people in power came from using that concept. He always said to look at, read, and study the Dred Scott case—and if we ever forgot, Dad would remind us kids that we were "less than a human being," by quoting from the decision.

I think my dad was more intellectually upset about racism than experiencing it—I never heard much about incidents from others in the family, either. He did give us a pretty good philosophy to grow on and make us strong—that we couldn't call ourselves Christian and think of any humans as not human.

At that time, the Democratic strength came out of the South, and it was an automatic thing for me not to like white Southerners. Those people across the board didn't like me. Now, I don't think that's prejudice because I was a good reader—their prejudice was wide open. To my dad, they had the Southern mind, the slave mind, they were the people who enslaved blacks, and the Democratic Party was their party.

But I guess I could be a little biased here. I do know good Southern people—William Faulkner out of Atlanta, Georgia, is one. I liked the reporting that came out of his paper, the *Atlanta Journal*. It sounded like something human to me.

Dad wasn't a Republican because he understood that they controlled the money like they do now, and there wasn't really any challenge to the white power structure. He wasn't persuaded by the Republicans' rhetoric—he looked at what they did with their money, what they did with their power, in education, for example, to keep people from equal opportunity.

I think Dad became attracted to the third parties that were a spilloff of all those radical things. I heard him talk about William Jennings Bryan, who was one Democrat he did support because he really raised hell for the little guy. Dad said he was not only a good talker, he knew what he was talking about.

My dad had seen the need to organize for the little guy with his own two eyes. He began to organize people in the 1910s because they weren't satisfied with the price of wheat. He felt, and a lot of others in Dakota County felt, we could make more money for wheat if not for the middleman.

But we were really organized around the issue of the creamery. We were shipping our milk to two creameries in the Twin Cities—the Modern creamery and the Quaker creamery. We'd bring the milk in five-, eight-, or ten-gallon cans. The train would pick up the milk every morning, and I was one of the main deliverers. I drove a team of horses at seven, and I was able to lift everything but the ten-gallon containers by the time I was ten. For the ten-gallon containers, I would tip them on their edge and roll them. Then we'd send it up to Minneapolis.

The Quaker creamery, I don't think it was run by Quakers, it just had the name, like Quaker Oats today. They cheated us just the same as everyone else. How they did it was, they cheated us on the weight of the milk, which they used to figure the percentage of cream in the butterfat. The cream level was not always the same, and it was just kind of hard to prove. How did we know they cheated us? Well, sometimes we weighed the ten-gallon containers first, unbeknownst to them. That was my idea, even as a little one, I was watchful. And of course their weights were lower.

Dad became one of the charter members of the Twin Cities Milk Producers Association, set up to counteract the middleman. With all the cheating going on, it didn't take much to organize those dairy farmers. He went ahead and did it without being named organizer because he felt it was for the good of the community. Dad never let up on a person he was trying to organize. People would get a little bit disgusted with me from time to time, so that rubbed off pretty good—just go for whatever it is that you want.

How did a black man organize mostly white farmers? The basis of that was Dad's ability to work for all people. The prejudice that you may have guessed was there at the time wasn't really there because all family-type farmers were not considered top-quality by the average person. When we came to the city, people would think, oh, those dumb farmers—you see it now with black people. The racism around is terrible when people look at you and regard themselves as superior in *any* way based on color. Then, it was also based on what you did.

Everybody knew Dad was black, but he didn't have that kind of skin—he was almost red. He had a very ruddy complexion year-round—like some white people in the summer, but he looked like that all the time. You see a bunch of farmers together, their complexions all look alike—real rough and red, more than tan. Most farmers did not lose that look for the winter months, either.

Part of him overcoming racial problems clearly was his intellect. He was a businessperson, educated to a point of knowing that all humanity should be treated right. Remember, Grandma Allen did educate all her kids to the tenth grade.

There were a lot of people in our community who were as humane as he was. The businesspeople in the farm towns all did business with us—there was no problem whatsoever. I don't think you should be amazed, given the history, and the activities of my father. When you get people active into the job and education situation, people know better, their intellect tells them not to do the wrong thing with us. I always thought that was the reason we never had problems. People knew us, knew we were involved and did good things. Everybody needed the creamery, things like that.

It was bound not to be missed by neighbors who would later vote for him for the school board and the township board. The farmers knew Dad was with them, too. He believed in a good education, and good health for people, and he acted on those things. It meant a lot if you could talk about the injustice of the price of milk.

Organizing the creamery required a hundred men at a hundred dollars a throw. I remember getting very upset at my dad writing a hundred-dollar check—I was concerned we would never get it back. I was ten or eleven, but I was very opinionated and very conservative with money. I had just started my first job—making fires at the school before it opened—so I was handling money and thought I knew everything.

I didn't really have the politics of people then, I was thinking more about money, but Dad had it right. Fortunately, I got the people part of the equation right soon enough.

I think it is not too blatant to say that my union work came out of my father's activity on the rights of the family-type farmer. I put the family farmer in the same class as labor, in terms of having to organize to fight power. My dad was never arrested. The danger was there, I think. There was something called the Palmer raids against labor people, radical farmers. People scared of going to jail for political thoughts. Some buried political materials, but we never did. J. Edgar Hoover, he was the chief of this witch hunt, and one committee after another in Congress.

But when Dad started the Twin Cities Milk Producers Association, it was about how the family farmer was cheated of milk. In Pine County, he was a founder of the Land O' Lakes co-op of Cloverdale. Together with all the other public service he did, that just meant a better living across the board for so many people.

I was just thinking about when he was in Dakota County, with the Milk Producers, we put through a railroad spur, just south of Orchard Gardens, which was called Oakdale. The railroad power structure out of St. Paul—I think it was Burlington at the time—they wanted to name it Allen's Spur, but the old man didn't want the publicity, because he was so low-key. We were large shippers of milk, and I'm sure the largest of hay. These were the things that provided economic development for so many people. You can see why I used him as my inspiration. Organizing was the right thing to do, and he just did it. So I did, too.

———

The Non-Partisan League erupted in North Dakota in 1915 and quickly spread to Minnesota; then, as now, struggling small farmers blamed the middleman for their plight. The NPL was the reaction—as one mid-century historian put it, "a movement, not a party . . . state socialism." The party was organized by Arthur C. Townley, a Browns Valley, Minnesota, flax farmer and fiery orator. Townley was not a socialist, believing that farmers would never support socialist principles. But Scandinavian immigrants, who came from collective societies, did not regard group action as a dirty word. On one level, the NPL worked like the modern interest group's political scorecard: the "movement" did not run candidates, but worked for them based on whether they supported such policies as state ownership of mills, packinghouses, and elevators; exempting farm improvements from taxation; and state hail insurance. But the NPL was

more than a grading system, attempting to organize and educate farmers
about economic empowerment. That was right up William Allen's furrow.

————————

Dad had some idea about organizing because politically, after Bryan, he just went over to the Non-Partisan League, which had a number of supporters, including the family farmers in Minnesota, especially on the western boundary of the state that was next to North Dakota. The Non-Partisan League was pretty much the family farmer organization early on, about getting up the price of wheat by fighting the middleman. In some parts of the Dakotas it was also about the price of beef. The platform called for equal pay for equal work, except that it bordered into production—that whatever you were producing, you should be getting what's fair from the so-called middlemen. I heard my father, as well as his neighbors, say over and over again, if we could just get those middle people, they control the prices.

The Non-Partisan League supported a lot of farm co-ops, the philosophy of putting co-ops and people together collectively to do great things. The first thing they did was change the tax structure—a lot of attorneys, a lot of well-heeled Republicans talked about taxing the co-ops. That was many, many years ago. The co-op movement was designed and started in Germany, and it was tax-exempt, which followed through in Minnesota.

That tax campaign speaks well to the Non-Partisan movement, because they kept it from being taxed. The Non-Partisan League believed in the rights of the family farmer and also in the rights of racial minorities. My father told me there was a lot of Non-Partisan League activity in Fergus Falls, Otter Tail County, where he traveled before settling down as a farmer.

One of the founders was a man by the name of Townley, a powerful organizer around the rights of all people to get an education. My father was quite a student of that and, later, organizing the family farmer. His focus on everyone getting a great education was all patterned after the Non-Partisan League.

1918: Pine County

Nellie Allen wakes on the morning
of her thirteenth birthday well before dawn
She hears her father already moving downstairs.
The wind is whining at the window,
Swirling new snow along the side
of the small house and by the barn below.
The cows are awake and waiting, she knows,
and the muskrat sets in the ditch must
to be checked before she leaves for school
in Hinckley, a long walk on a winter's day

The white kitchen table is covered
with broadsides from the night before.
William Allen, home from a meeting
of the Non-partisan League,
is full of ideas to get better prices
for small farmers, although he knows
that the railroad companies in St. Paul
and the milk buyers in Minneapolis
will use their money and influence
to try to stop them. "It just isn't right,"
her father says. "It's just not right at all."

Gladys Foree Allen, a teacher from Kentucky and his wife,
stirs the grits boiling on the wood stove.
"Nellie," she says, "take these pamphlets with you
this morning. Drop one at each farm and at each house
in town. People should know what's going on!"

"Yes, Mama," her daughter answers, picking one up.
And in the dim light of the gas lantern,
Nellie begins to read.

From "Nellie at Ninety"
(Robert L. Carothers, 1995)

I remember Dad had me pinned to the saddle at thirteen doing Non-Partisan League work. I was doing the distribution of literature to the farmers. I kept that horse walking so I could read! I just propped the material up on the saddlehorn to read it.

> I remember one day [when I was ten years old], shortly after we moved up [to Pine County], my assignment for some kind of class, a school class, was to make this presentation and the idea hit me; I knew exactly what I want to do. I wanted to talk about "Big Biz," out of the Non-Partisan League paper.
>
> So I came home that day and I said to my mother, where is that paper? She said, "What paper are you talking about?" You know, that paper that we get here every week or whatever, the one with "Big Biz" in it. She said, "Come here, young lady. You notice that comes to us in a plain brown wrapper? There are some things you don't talk about and you're not going to take that to school and discuss what's in that paper." I couldn't understand the reasoning at the time but as I got older I believed what she told me was quite funny, kind of underground movement. (MHS, 3)

———

Later, the Non-Partisan League gave way to more organized political parties, including the Farmer-Labor Party in Minnesota. Floyd Bjorstjerne Olson, a former radical longshoreman, was the party's breakthrough governor in 1930, propelled by his economic populism and his reputation as a corruption-busting County Attorney in Hennepin County, where Minneapolis is located. He proposed unemployment insurance, a progressive income tax, pensions, and expanded environmental protection. He planned to run for the U.S. Senate in 1936, proposing federal ownership of national industrial monopolies. But he died in the middle of that year from stomach cancer, just forty-four years old. A memorable Olson quote: "I do not mind being called a 'red' . . . I would prefer it to the term 'yellow.'"

———

The Non-Partisan League was a people kind of thing that the Farmer-Labor Party in Minnesota was based on. I don't remember the differences, they seemed more similar, but with the NPL more geared toward the farm. The Non-Partisan League was more of a movement to begin with, but the Farmer-Laborers were people that needed a political party to show their power. Some of the differences, early on, basically came back to equality of people. Who learned from who—the NPL was there first, based on equality of the family-type farmer—but my family believed in carrying it further, constitutionally speaking, to everybody, so that led to the Farmer-Labor Party.

If I remember right, the philosophy of the Non-Partisan League rubbed off on the Progressives in Wisconsin to formulate the same party around those issues. The treatment of ordinary human beings, the cooperative movement, the family-type farmer making a better life. I remember a lot of the same things coming into their platforms.

Dad supported Bob La Follette [Wisconsin's Progressive Party leader] when he came into politics. Old Bob La Follette, when he was governor, he had the best labor school in the country. He knew the philosophy.

For Dad, Bob La Follette was next to God and so was the great Minnesota Farmer-Labor governor Floyd B. Olson. That was because both spoke out on the family farm issues, on the workers' issues. They had me on horseback in 1919, 1920, handing out material door-to-door for the Farmer-Labor Party when I was fourteen and fifteen. The Farmer-Laborers were sending people to Congress and the Senate by then. One of the first big Farmer-Labor winners was Floyd B. Olson, who I think was Hennepin County Attorney first before he became governor.

Because there wasn't a Farmer-Labor presidential candidate, I think Dad voted for the Socialist Norman Thomas for president in 1928 and I think he voted for the Communist Eugene Debs the year he got one million votes [1920].

That's how radical my dad was: William Jennings Bryan, Norman Thomas, Gene Debs. To my dad, they all supported good, equal opportunity in education, good training in jobs, and the family farm. There was nothing scary about them, except to the power structure of racism and money.

One way Dad was able to do things was he was just very strong in the field of human development. He got to know people when he operated in Dakota County. The Dan Patch railroad went through Lakeville, and Dad would be gone three hours or so at a time to talk with members of the International Workers of the World, who were mostly railroad people. He strongly identified with anyone who was intelligent and not like everybody else. If anybody told the old man there was a Jew within a radius of a hundred miles, he'd get there, just take off and go talk, set up a relationship. I think he was lonesome for political talk. There were only so many people out there in the country. He went up to Minneapolis lots of times, too.

I suppose the reason Dad cared about reaching out to Jews is that it was where Dad was, intellectually. He said, "I've got to go over there and talk to this man, we understand each other." As I got older, I understood the parallels between anti-Semitism and racism. He just didn't like anyone treating anyone differently, and we heard a lot of anti-Jewish comments in those days. Our neighbors to the north in Lakeville, the Straniks—other neighbors would refer to them as Christ killers.

I can't reconcile the lack of racist comments versus anti-Semitic comments in Lakeville. That's just how it was. The Catholics, an awful lot of Catholic Irish people, were on the side of the Yankees in the Civil War, and didn't see much harm in blacks. But I guess some didn't feel that way about Jews. I'm sure that was it—you find a lot of people split that way.

One Jewish man Dad talked to was the town blacksmith—I remember going to the shop to see the bellows and machinery. When we lived in Pine County, my father visited another Jewish person, just to talk—he worked on a farm outside of Danbury, Wisconsin. We would ride horses and when the roads were dry, we took out a Tin Lizzy. Danbury was fourteen or fifteen miles from Pine County. He made it a point to know everybody and judge the philosophy of where they were coming from.

There was a livestock dealer in Hinckley named Weedess. He and Dad would talk about black-Jewish unity. This man and my dad tried to bring my brother Richard up to snuff on black-Jewish relations. Richard didn't read as much as the rest of us in the family. Dad really wanted to make him understand the anti-Semitism that existed for two thousand years, and make it parallel to the situation with blacks.

Dad also would buy dozens of caps and gloves at Kaplan Brothers on Franklin Avenue, because they were great supporters of human rights for all people. Kaplan Brothers was a large store in south Minneapolis, with all-over-the-place tables. It was at Fifteenth and Franklin for years. We bought a lot of overalls, work shoes, and work gloves. When Dad came in, he didn't buy one or two, he bought by the dozens—it was as if he was furnishing a workingperson's store himself. We went through a lot of Kaplan Brothers merchandise because we were working hard all the time.

Dad could also tell lots of people his ideas because he was addicted to ice cream. How does ice cream have anything to do with it? Well, we had a two-gallon ice cream freezer, which he ordered from Sears—he was a stockholder—and he'd make two gallons at a time and have the whole county out to the farm.

Of course, it wasn't much of a machine—the machine power was me and my brother. I remember how much work we did trying to get ice cream frozen for Santa Claus. Dad would do the Santa Claus thing, and he'd dutifully take a bowl of ice cream, so we'd get up and find a bowl gone. We made it with a cooked custard—good things, since eggs carried bacteria. We added milk and cream for freezing.

Because he was such a leader, my dad was elected to the Dakota County School Board in 1913. He was elected in Hinckley, too. In our old Pine County kitchen, there was always a coffee pot on the stove. I heard a lot there through my father talking to everyone in the community at our kitchen table over a cup of coffee.

Dad supported education across the board, probably because *his* mother believed in it across the board, and I did it across the board. There was another overlapping on our experiences: I went onto the state college board, he was on the school district board.

With Dad's background, of course, he would have run for higher office had he been white. He got elected and had close friendships with other men in the community, but he was a very sensible person and figured if he ran for too high an office, that would have brought out the racial stuff, especially with more strangers voting.

I'm sure he was frustrated about it at times, but he never shared it with us. He just had to have been, given his own intelligence of things. You knew what he knew about the political atmosphere. The stymieing factors were there—like with me when I ran in the forties. I knew what I would run up against, and I had two factors against me: I was a woman and was supposed to be a moron because I was black.

In the late 1920s, the Democratic Party became more populist. In 1928, the party nominated Al Smith, governor of New York, the first Catholic nominee and one who might appeal to immigrants who shared his religion. Then, in 1932, came another New York governor, Franklin D. Roosevelt, who announced a "New Deal" of government-funded stimulus programs to jumpstart the depression economy. Among Roosevelt's farthest-reaching initiatives was the Rural Electrification Administration (REA), which provided struggling farms with inexpensive power. The Farm Credit Administration provided lower-cost loans to get through the economic crisis. One of FDR's main lieutenants was Harold R. Ickes, a Chicago lawyer and secretary of the interior. FDR's vice president in 1940 was Henry A. Wallace, an Iowa editor, agronomist, and political leftist who ran with the Progressive Party in 1948, advocating equal rights for all minorities, price and rent controls, and curbs on the powers of monopolies.

There never seemed to be a time at home that there were not people there at the kitchen table, talking about some political issue that affected their lives. It was the town meeting place, for the school board, the town board, the Rural Electrification Board. My father was active in all those things, and he was appointed to the Rural Electrification Board by old Harold Ickes, of FDR's administration. He was one of the first appointees. Ickes was President Roosevelt's right-hand man. Dad didn't really know Ickes, but Ickes knew him by reputation in the education field and by his political activities. Roosevelt took a lot of ideas from the Non-Partisan League, and I think Ickes got a list of Minnesota members that Dad was on.

The funny thing about Dad was that in a picture of the two, his picture showed up much whiter than Harold Ickes—he had a very ruddy complexion. Everybody, including FDR and Eleanor, had made a ruckus about Dad representing equal opportunity, and some New Dealers also talked him up as a poor farmer, to show how they were bringing in all classes of people.

We didn't see it that way. Dad managed the farm in a way that we had whatever we wanted! What happened, I guess, was that in this part of the state, the more northern part where the soil wasn't quite as good, they were in a dollar kind of way considered poor. But at the same time, we could buy and sell most of those people who are poor now! My mother would turn over in her grave if she heard me say we weren't poor. Even though we ate well, had an automobile, a telephone, teams of horses, she'd still say we were poor people. I guess it was good to keep the kids' feet on the ground!

Dad began his turn toward the Democrats under Al Smith, when the Democrats nominated him for president in 1928. That's when I noticed the politics of my parents and grandparents changing. We were one of the few people supporting Al Smith, who a lot of the Irish Catholics liked.

I don't know if Dad knowingly became a Democrat. He was working for Al Smith and he was running on a Democrat platform. Those old-timers made their own platforms. FDR, I remember him as governor of New York, and by 1932, I was beginning to see the history of what they were doing and the move toward equal opportunity and equal pay.

You see the embodiment of what is humanly good and proper, and then somebody comes along of different political persuasion and embraces those things, so you support him. That's just smart—if the chance of winning is there, you can't be old-fashioned about what their party did before if there is real, fundamental change.

My dad saw that his ideals were preserved and expanded by Governor Roosevelt. He was involved in Al Smith's campaign when it was embracing opportunity for all people, so Democrats were something to take another look at.

Later, when the Democrats attached themselves to very radical politics, then Dad was almost always a Democrat. But that didn't mean the old Democrats, the slave people. It was like Colin Powell, who called himself a Republican, but I heard the media quiz him, and he took the whole Humphrey platform, the FDR program; he had taken it as his own—the liberal platform of Democrats after 1928. He talked about fair housing, equal opportunity across the board, even mentioned equal opportunity for women, that was definitely from Roosevelt—should we say Eleanor?

The New Deal turned out to be a natural for Dad. His political history—he worked with the Farm Credit Administration, as well as the REA. They suspected him of being a radical politician because of the Non-Partisan League. But those kinds of political jobs were available if you were willing to work, and with his reputation it was no problem. My father practically lived in Pine City in the thirties, and the REA board met over in Finlayson. Some of the younger members of the family were kind of resentful that he was away from milking so much.

Dad was there when anything pertained to the family farm—the amount of interest you could charge on mortgage-type funds, the Rural Credit Administration, health and education programs. Younger people sometimes have a hard time fitting into the issues of the day, but the Farm Credit Administration was about us right then, right now. We always felt the money men were cheating the family farmer and worker. My father was one of the few successful farmers who supported labor, who understood economics and the role the family farmer was playing in overall human development.

Some of my brothers and sisters were jealous of the ties between Dad and me, and the attention I ended up getting in my life, but to give you the honest truth about me, I never had time to be jealous of anyone else. The one brother I have left, Cortland, he's not jealous, because he's also very busy with his business.

My brothers and sisters didn't pay as much attention to politics, maybe because everybody was younger. I probably said to myself a hundred times, how could anyone miss that in our family, where our bread and butter was coming from, how the organizations play a role in their life? I look at the number of people who are antilabor in high schools today, in various four-year and two-year colleges, just because they have enough to eat. You just have to experience it, I guess. My dad and I blazed a lot of the trails, so maybe my brothers and sisters didn't experience it like I did.

Chapter 5

Mom

I did not worship my mother quite like my father. It wasn't lovey-dovey between me and her, but I respected her. I think I looked down on her a bit because she was sickly a lot.

She didn't feel good and was pregnant most of the time. A couple of the early kids were quite large—Herbert was one of them. He was born fifteen pounds. Frankly, I don't know how she got by me; I was thirteen pounds—no wonder she hurt. I thank God that she ended up having smaller babies. Gladys, if I remember right, was seven and a half to eight pounds, and Cortland and Clemmy were the same. Mom gave birth to nine kids, and the folks raised seven of us. I used to say I would not be like my mother, pregnant all the time. In our family, being born was a little bit different than in other families. Our mother always tried to use a doctor for her births. In Dakota County, there was a woman from England, Mrs. Leonard, who assisted with all of her births except Almeda. Mrs. Leonard could cook almost as good as my mother. You could judge by breads and cinnamon rolls—they almost tasted like Mother's.

We always called her the nurse; she teamed up with Dr. Gaffney from Lakeville. We used professionals right from the get-go, then to back it up, we used Mrs. Leonard. She was a traditional English-type lady, a little on the heavy side, who lived four or five miles from us. When we got her, we always went after her with the horse and buggy, and then with the old Ford car. She was apparently very good, because she was contracted by the calendar, by when babies arrived. There was some overlapping—we'd call and one of her sons would say, she's at Mrs. So-and-So's house, so you did the best you could until she got the other mother out of the way.

There was one time when she couldn't reach us, and my father's mother did the birth—we sent for Grandma Allen. She lived on the north shore of Crystal Lake then, near our second Dakota County farm. All I know is she went through the birth, and she was able to do what the midwife or doctor would do. You have to remember that Grandma had birthed nine kids herself.

My feelings about Mom being sick, that wasn't purely a resentment of her, it was just how things were. I had to help her with the stuff I liked doing least, then help her even more with it when she got sick. Mom didn't feel very good, she wasn't as strong, and she couldn't do that constant work, cooking three meals a day, washing all those clothes.

The heaviest part of her load was cooking and keeping the house clean. We did have a woman come out to wash the week's clothes because of all the cooking Mom had to do. The bread was one of the hardest chores, because she baked every other day, ten to twelve loaves. It was just hard work, kneading, it was tedious. Aside from us, we also had two hired men on the farm to feed. We'd take guys eighteen, nineteen, twenty, sometimes twenty-two years old. My dad used to say it's a bottomless pit, eat, eat, eat. He was a heavy eater, too—he was big, not fat.

I didn't like cooking and housekeeping, but I liked to eat, so I learned to make good cakes and breads, and fairly good pies, I guess. I was pretty strong, and I liked good bread, so I did the kneading a lot. But I would miss school sometimes to catch up at home, and I never wanted to miss a day of school, so I suppose I took it out on Mom if I did. It was harder to get me to do housework than farm work. I liked being in the field, I liked to plow.

I'm sure I did think, Oh, if Mom were healthy, this wouldn't happen to me. I was in my teens then, and the teenage years are probably the cruelest time of one's life.

Here's another factor that might surprise you about the problems between Mom and me: she was an academic, and in those years, academic-type people were not as highly thought of in the community, either. Maybe some of that might have rubbed off on me, even though I was a rock-solid believer in education. How do I explain that? I don't know. I do remember the attitude of people toward academics. You hear people say things like "you educated fool"—I guess I was then old enough to equate that to what my mother was. The older you get, the more you try to analyze where your beliefs come from.

I guess the part that rubbed off on me was that higher education didn't always mean common sense. I mean, my dad was intelligent and commonsensical, but he only went to the tenth grade. My mom graduated from college! I could've been conflicted a little bit about educational matters.

The other thing not to discount is the basic troubles mothers and daughters can have. I think moms get caught in the crossfire a bit. Dad's outside, running to meetings, whereas Mother was hemmed into house and kids, so you find yourself arguing with mothers about the daily things you want to do. Very little argument went on with Dad—you just didn't try, he had that air.

When Mom was sick, Grandmother Allen did help out from time to time. In Pine County, we built my grandparents a house at the south end of the Hinckley farm, which meant half a mile away from our house. We put in a phone, so she was subject to two shorts and a long [rings], but she couldn't walk that distance when she got older— remember, this was a *big* woman. I'd have to bring her up. She did oversee the cooking from time to time, but couldn't go through it every day, even when Mom was sick.

I met Grandma Allen the first time three years before they moved to Minnesota to live with us in Dakota County. It was 1911 or 1912, when she was forty-seven and I was six. She'd never seen me before then, but we corresponded often. We were mailing stuff back and forth—Grandma wrote every day to somebody, I found that out after she came to Minnesota to live on our farm, in 1914. I wrote to her about whatever happened, that I got a new cat, a new litter of pigs, when I started riding a horse. I remember my mother told me once, "I don't know how she handled everything you sent."

I liked Grandma. Most kids like their grandmas if they're a little bit fat. I always felt so secure with my parents, but it was nice when both of my father's parents came to live with us. Grandma Allen was a good cook; I should have known because she was kind of heavy. I remember when she came to live at our farm, I put her on the scale, because she was big and I wanted to find out how big she was. I remember the scale didn't act right because I didn't put the right weights on it, but it turned out she was about three hundred pounds. Dad had to come over and he said, "You need to put another weight"—I had a hundred-pound weight on there, but I needed two hundred pounds! I don't know how I talked her into it—it could've been my mouth, I was pretty good with it at times. I could've sold her a bill of goods. I know I was a very curious child.

She read all the time. Of course, on Sunday morning, she made sure we read a lot of passages in the Bible. I wasn't too disciplined about reading the Bible—I liked the history, but the other part of it, the religious part, I wasn't too good about that. Still, if I missed Sunday school I was fit to be tied, because I was missing the history of the Bible. I don't know why I wasn't tuned in to the religious part at such an early age.

Grandma Allen was also a stern woman, stern on things that had to do with chores, keeping clothes clean. By time she got up here, I was nearly ten, old enough to wash our clothes. We had old-fashioned washing machines, with the cranks. I wasn't too big on doing that chore, and she knew it, so she was always on me to do it.

I don't know what happened there, why they moved up with us in Lakeville. They had sold off their horse and cows, and had a place in town in Missouri for a while. My feeling is that my grandfather Allen got into problems with a lady. I guess I probably wouldn't call her a lady—Grandma certainly didn't.

Anyway, my grandparents wanted seven or eight cows of their own in Lakeville, to sell a little milk. They bought these cows, and Dad gave them a team of horses, two brood mares. I remember how hard it was to get them on the telephone. I had to call Lakeville, and the operator there had to call Farmington, she had to call Rosemount. One day I heard the operators talking to each other; one finally said, "What's all that racket on the line?" and the other said, "Oh, that's that Allen girl, trying to get her grandma to make a birthday cake."

Grandma said she was too busy getting ready for Christmas to bake me a cake. My birthday was December seventeeth. My mother said, "I tell you what—your birthday is close to Christmas, and I had a brother born on Christmas Day," so she said, "we'll just celebrate them all together," and I just threw a fit. I knew I had been had!

Grandfather Allen was pretty nice, not as stern, particularly to the younger kids. He loved younger kids—there was nothing they'd ask for that he wouldn't give. It upset all ends of the family, including father and mother. You know how some grandparents are—he was typical. Grandpa, he couldn't do a whole lot, because he was getting older.

Later on, my grandmother was only about sixty-five, sixty-six, or something like that, and so the folks put her on the school board in Pine County. I just had it all the way, one generation after the other of activists. (MHS, 2)

I don't want to leave you with the wrong impression of my mother as an invalid, or a fool. My mother was a great force when it came to history—she was as much of a history buff as I am.

My mother was a very good school teacher. I was thinking the other day about history, and my mother used to [tell] me, "You're reading this about yourself: 'you're lazy, you're no good, you're all of these bad things, void of intelligence.' Learn it for your examination, but the real history is thus and so . . ." And I think that really conditioned me right off the reel. (MHS, 2)

She could draw a picture of everybody participating in history, of what their attitude and philosophy were. She was talking to me about a lot of things that I was not old enough to comprehend, but I can remember the mental pictures of what she drew with her mind, her stories. My mother and I didn't get along perfectly, but it wasn't that bad, because I learned a lot of history.

I believe history is so important because learning history—especially if it's of any nationality that has been enslaved or counted as second class—will cause young people's intellect not to be enslaved out of a similar situation. The Irish and other people weren't treated right. History helps people be something other than what they were. People don't want to be slaves, they know some people might still treat them like slaves, but they will know about that and recognize that and say, what's wrong with me being like you! And some of the children of slave masters don't want to be that, either!

To some extent, we all are defined by our ancestors, and we'd better know about it. I think there's a cultural identity there, some things that you want to hang on to and some things you want to get rid of to be that well-rounded human being you want to be. I just wanted equality in anything I went after—no brakes on me going to school, or in the literary learning part of things, or what kind of work I could do, or what I could be trained for if I liked it.

Mom worked the farm's gardens most of the time—we had one- to two-acre gardens, very big, in both Dakota and Pine County. In Pine County, Mom had ten to fifteen rhubarb plants—which makes a *lot* of rhubarb. We started out the season with green beans, perennials like rhubarb, and at one end of the garden we had hot beds, which is where we grew tomato plants from seed—beets, and cabbage, to have as early food. The big hot beds—they were like miniature hothouses, with wood around them, containing nicely treated soil which you spaded up early on. You'd put glass on top to get the heat on top, then there's the heat from the hot bed of manure underneath. There was condensation from the glass, which just did tremendous things for keeping the ground moist. We'd plant plants with a month, and month and a half growth.

The other food up there was beans, navy beans—I still love 'em. We always had our own meat; we put up ham, bacon, fresh pork every season. My mother had a strong stable formula for preserving things. It didn't make any difference if she put things up in half-gallon jars; every season, she'd do a hundred quarts of corn, a hundred quarts of green beans, a hundred quarts of blueberries and tomatoes, and as close to a hundred quarts of rhubarb as she could get. Plus pickles and sauerkraut—she'd put that stuff down there by the barrel. The only thing we really had to buy was sugar and flour.

That was a big reason the depression wasn't hard—we didn't even know it was a depression on the farm. We could still eat and we could still sell. We didn't have debts we couldn't pay. Just about everybody except us and the Irons family in Pine County had some trouble. The Irons were like us in their ability to grow stuff and put it away. Lots of families didn't plan, or didn't produce during the summertime, or they didn't have cows. We did have silage that we stored to tide over price swings.

Again, people think the depression blew everybody apart. It's a part of not knowing those pockets of history, taking too much the clichés of history, like all black families were poor or ignorant. There were families around that did fine, regular families. The old man was very involved in the New Deal getting things organized, so that the average farmer did not feel the hard pangs about what the depression produced.

I'm trying to get communities of color, and the Native American people out from under the yoke of clichéd discrimination—taking for granted all the clichés, lazy, dirty, that they won't do this and that. *All* of the clichés are evil. That's one reason I'm doing this book.

Chapter 6

School Days

My schoolhouse in Lakeville was a one-room schoolhouse, first to eighth grade. I would say there were closer to fifty kids in that schoolhouse. It was nice hardwood on the inside, and we had a great big drum-covered stove that sat at one end of the room. I thought it was a great school because my dad ordered the stove, from St. Paul Book and Stationery. Of course, my brother Richard and I felt everything he did was right.

In that school, there was one teacher I remember, a woman from Hastings, named Katy Hynes. I just thought she was a good teacher—she'd raise Cain with me every once in a while. I was a good student but I was stubborn. There was only one teacher for us all, so it was tough.

I was not the smartest kid in that school at first, but I was kind of an animal, I could work any problem at math to death. By the time I was fifteen, I was good. I loved history, I liked reading. That math thing did come because I liked work. We weren't short on any reading matter at home, and if you just read the ads, if nothing else, you're likely to smarten up a little bit. The farm had a lot to do with me getting smart at math—the price of land, the price of crops, put that all together.

I started reading fairly early, at about five, I was looking at pictures. The first thing I remember reading—I remember it because I was really struggling with the words—was the first-grade reader. Then the *Minneapolis Tribune* cover to cover, mostly pictures at first, but then I tried to read it.

At eight, I read my first novel. Well, it wasn't a novel, but it was a book about four girls called *Dandelion's Cottage*. They just ke[ ] little house in the summer, renting it out, and one day, befo[ ] the house for the fall, they put on a very lavish dinner and in[ ] old man and woman they liked best of all. After this meal, they found out the old people were a brother and sister who hadn't spoken for years. I liked that format—doing something good without being totally aware of what it was, all because they liked people. I was that oddball who was always buried in a book or papers. I would go to the field or a barn with certain parts of the paper folded in my pocket.

I read recipes, the style pattern page, and then every once in a while some little flappy story about animals. As a kid, of course, animals took on the stature of human beings. I never liked dolls—just give me a book. There was a Christmas song, Santa Claus is packing his bag, visiting all the families, well, there's a part talks about "Nellie likes books, thinks dolls are folly." They're not talking about me, but they are talking about me, if you know what I mean.

We weren't short on reading material around my house. We had the *Clapper Farmer* and *Wallace's Farmer*—Henry Wallace. I supported him for president in 1948 on the Progressive ticket, his father was the publisher. The local publication was simply called the *Farmer*. There was also the *Farm Stock and Home*. As for black papers, we got the *Chicago Defender* every week, and another paper out of St. Louis. We came by reading honestly—Grandma Allen taught reading and writing.

The *Minneapolis Morning Tribune* came every day. When they were building the *Titanic,* I remember them reading that they were talking about it being invincible. My mom told me just before the ship set sail that this was a ship that was not supposed to sink.

We got our telephone in 1912. What happens in small towns like Lakeville is that cablegrams came in to tell the town the news. The night the *Titanic* sank, the cablegrams came into the Cities, and those operators would then call up everybody on the party line. Our line was twenty-eight people, so the gal from Lakeville had to call twenty-eight people. In Hinckley, Pine County, we had an alert for everyone on the line, a certain ring for everyone to pick up the line.

My first job outside of the farm was making fires at the Lakeville schoolhouse before school. School was only a mile away, and I drove our car down there because Dad needed the horses to work. I had started driving when I was seven—no one thought much about kids driving then, cars were so new.

I lobbied for that job—I guess that was my first successful lobbying job. See, I had an in because my father was on the school board, but he said to me, you go see the other school board members. The first one I went to said, "Nellie, you've always been a responsible lady"—well, that was such a thing for me to hear at ten! I always thought so but to hear it from someone else! I was in District Ninety-three at that time. Don't forget, I was much older in my head than my actual age.

I got paid five dollars a month to make the fires—that was heap big stuff—but I wouldn't go into the woodshed until the other kids got there. I was scared someone would get me! I never talked to my parents about this. What I did to do the job was, the night before, I would take kindling, pour some oil on it, and use that to start the school fire so I wouldn't have to spend so much time in that cold empty building. I was scared to death, but I did it anyway. That's me.

I mostly couldn't wait to leave to go to school. When I had to miss a day, for farmwork or housework, I'd jump up and down and cry and carry on. Mom often wasn't feeling up to par. I had to help her clean house and take some care of her. I remember we had this milk separator, we had to wash the pieces every morning—a hundred and twenty little disks. They would separate the cream from the milk, like pasteurization. Oh, it was terrible—I missed so many days it made me mad! I know that was selfish, but I just enjoyed school so.

The school in Pine County was actually in Clover Township, which was fourteen miles one way—I'd never have gotten through high school without the bus. My father drove the bus. Well, we called it the van—we were still in the horse-and-buggy days when he started driving it around Pine County. A lot of it was getting kids from eighth grade to the high school. It was horse-drawn, and I remember one day

Dad said we had to have faster horses, other than the heavy draft horses. So we ended up using two teams, one every other day.

In Pine County we were the only black family again. It was another one-room school, a little bigger than in Dakota County. We had books in Dakota County, but here they had a little partitioned-off area with books. The stove was another big stove, and then there was a corner where they put a partition and shelves for a little library. It was nice—I liked that little library, it was probably ten feet by six. It was no different being black in Pine County than in Dakota. The fact that Dad was again involved in the running of the school, I think that eased it. There could've been problems if we were not so active maybe.

He was on the board, one of the ones people looked to for what policy we should have. He and my grandma were two of the ones who brought in two years of high school. The old high school in Hinckley was fourteen miles away. I attempted it, but the roads were too bad. I didn't like driving the car, I needed a scoop shovel for snow and mud. It was a Model T, and I drove it myself when my dad didn't drive me. I made a few trips to the Hinckley school.

In order to add the two years of high school in Clover Township, you needed the OK from the state Department of Education. My father and Grandma Allen lobbied the State Board to get it. It wasn't the first time my dad had lobbied—my first trip to the capitol in St. Paul was when I was eight years old, in Dakota County, when he went to the legislature to get more state aid for students. At the time, it sure wasn't much—he got the board together to ask that state aids be made seventy-five dollars per student, up from sixty-five dollars.

The capitol just flabbergasted me. The only thing I didn't like was the steps, which were cold and icy because the legislature mostly meets during the winter. But I thought the building was really something. We were treated well, as I remember. I didn't know anybody, of course, and people were running here and there, stopping everybody on steps. I remember my dad and I did stop at one of the lunch counters because he wanted coffee. I wanted to know what everybody was doing—it was very amazing and inspiring. I didn't make up my mind to run for office at that time; I just wanted to know what was going on.

We had to come up on the Dan Patch railroad, which ran to the Cities from Orchard Lake and Northfield. We got on at Orchard Gardens. The old man let me go to the fruit stores on Seventh Street in Minneapolis. Back then, from Sixth Avenue back to First Avenue North, one store after another sold fruit, and he let me buy as many bananas as I could handle. I could see bananas hanging in the window from the station, and I said I had to have bananas. He gave me some money and said, "Get some for the kids." I still remember those bananas.

Dad's involvement also affected my social life. I liked dancing on the farm—we had barn dancing. There was also a school that hadn't been occupied for a while, the town hall, we'd go there. I liked the circle two-step, the old-fashioned square dancing, I even learned to do a waltz from the old-timers. The whole countryside turned out. See, in Hinckley, there were many townships and they had their own hall— many times for having dances. Clover Township wasn't different. My father didn't dance, but other men did.

There was no alcohol, a lot of lemonade, cake, and ice cream. Most of the time we used a neighbor who was fiddle player. And Mr. Robertson was one of the teachers up there—from Mora, Minnesota, not too far from us—but he was a good fiddler. We'd have people come from miles around, thirty-five to fifty people. Even though we had a big room for dancing in, at times it seemed kind of crowded. Sometimes, we'd have 'em like every other weekend, and sometimes, every week in between—usually in colder weather when people weren't working as much. Of course, my father would get us up to do milking the next morning.

— Chapter 7 —

Off to the Big City

Tenth grade was as far as school went up in Clover Township. If I wanted to go on for two more years of high school, Hinckley was fourteen miles away, and I did just not want to drive that Ford car to get there.

I really didn't like driving the car because in the spring the road was muddy, and I didn't like the ice and snow either. I'd carry a five-gallon milk can of alcohol to keep the radiator from freezing. I remember once when I was in my twenties, I was up at the farm for a while when my mother was ill, and I was going to some political meeting, I think it was a Unitarian meeting in Askov, Minnesota, which is nearby. Well, when I got there, I reeked of alcohol.

I had a vivid opinion about leaving home. I was going to finish up my high school education at the University of Minnesota; that was more common then, through their extension side. Nobody wanted me to go to Minneapolis—my father and mother didn't want me to go. But there was no argument; I just wanted to continue school. My parents made the argument many times that I should stay at home and go to Hinckley High School, but they knew how hard it was for me to get there. The ride was so bad that lots of girls from my area left Sunday night and stayed in Hinckley until Friday. There was a Mrs. Fry in Hinckley; she boarded most all of the farm girls for miles around. She had ten to twelve rooms in that big old house.

To be able to leave, I just kept talking—talking and yelling and carrying on. I bugged my parents half to death. I wanted to learn everything

59

I could learn, and I couldn't do it there. I knew that was a soft spot for them, because of how much they believed in education, and that's why they never told me outright not to go. They didn't give me any arguments, but they said, we'll see, we'll see.

It was kind of a split thing in me, because I knew my mom was ill, and she needed me for heavy things around the house. At seventeen, I couldn't keep up with all that needed to be done. It was rough—Cortland, Clemmy, and Almeda were all in school, and the old man was busy, in the winter he was cutting ice off Crystal Lake and Orchard Lake. He survived because the older boys weren't around the house, so he didn't have to take care of them, and Cortland, Clem, and Almeda, they were getting to the point where they took care of themselves. There were some things no one else around the house could do as well as I—washing and cooking; I did that since I was ten years old.

They never said they needed me more here, but I could tell by the other arguments they gave me. They said all cities are dangerous places for young girls to go to, but I always felt I could fight my way out of everything. Of course, that wasn't true. I never realized then how bad it could be, sexual harassment.

I came to the city, Minneapolis, in September 1922, after helping all through the summer to put up barrels of sweet pickles. I had to work to get out of there! We used these great hardwood barrels for the pickles, and I remember doing fifty-five-gallon barrels of sauerkraut. There was no shortage of food when I left. I remember I sewed myself two dresses that summer—not what city people wore as far as style, but they'll do.

I didn't think it was that bad moving here at all. I had a job when I came down to the Cities. I was taking care of an apartment and three kids on Spruce Place, right by Loring Park in Minneapolis. One child was seven and the other was almost a teenager, plus there was another baby. They were white, and I lived with them. I slept on a roll-away in their apartment. There were too many people in that apartment! There was only one bedroom, and I slept in the back hallway. It was good only because the apartment had two entrances. I had to leave that family because the baby cried all night.

I had gotten the job through the church we went to, Bethesda Baptist. Mrs. Helm was one of the founders of the church, and she got me the job with this white family, and a second family, too.

The second job involved two older kids, teenage girls. We were close to the same age; we'd go out and walk, and go over to Loring Park. They liked to play tennis a little bit. I didn't know the game, but I was much stronger, so I did OK. Their mom gave us money to go over to the Orpheum to see movies. These were thirteen- and fourteen-year-old girls, and I remember thinking, I was taking care of a whole family at that age! This place wasn't far from the first place I lived at on Spruce Place.

One day, after a big dinner of roast turkey on a Sunday with my uncle Clarence and aunt Della in North Minneapolis, I just stayed all night, and then I just decided to stay for good. I told that second family I had been living with that I didn't want to stay, and the woman didn't have a fit about it. I wasn't a natural nanny or babysitter. It was not my natural calling to cook and make breakfast for them. Even so, it wasn't as hard as farmwork. Here, we had power machines, like an engine to run the washing machine.

My uncle's apartment was a flat, a five-room apartment—three bedrooms, a living room/dining room, and a fairly large kitchen. All with good hardwood. There was a piano in the living room, good furniture, and rugs. It wasn't really a big change from home—except we had linoleum back home and six or eight kids running around!

The great piece in my aunt's living room was their Victrola. We really cranked it up when we put records on. I remember our neighbors back in Lakeville got one before there were flat records—they had a cylinder that made the sounds. The thing I'll never forget about that Victrola was the little dog they used to sell it—listening in to hear his master's voice. The thing that interested me was that this little needle brought a voice out!

There were a lot of mom-and-pop businesses on both sides of the block on Sixth Avenue North, a lot of Jewish business owners. You know the old saying about when you get three Jews together, you've got an argument. Well, the same is true when you get two blacks together. So that was a lively place. It's right where Olson Memorial Highway is now.

My uncle's apartment was right over the People's Bakery. The bakery was two units, with a billiard room right on the corner of Jewitt and Olson Highway.

You remember the smells. I could smell bread when they first started making it at five A.M., the Jewish bread, with the braided top—what do you call that? Challah? The Viennese bread, those loaves were all the same, heavy European doughs. When the loaves were coming out of the oven, I was there to pick up my loaf.

The billiard room was a rough place—a lot of young Jewish males arguing with each other. They were playing cards, though we were not supposed to know that. My uncle said they were coming to fight because they were playing cards, and that was a natural result. Their format was like black billiard rooms and club rooms on Bryant all the way to Lyndale. Between young Jews and blacks, there was plenty of activity. People today don't think that the two groups are very similar, but they were both on the low end of the totem pole, and there was plenty of discrimination toward each group, so there was a lot of anger and a lot of scrapping and criminality.

Every other place on our block was a business of some kind, usually Jewish owned. On Colfax there was a black grocery story, and on Bryant, another black-owned grocery. I didn't know too much about those groceries, because I shopped mostly at the Jewish grocery stores nearby. There was quite a large barbershop on the block, and a delicatessen, with a couple more across the street.

I took to the area right away because it was a convenient thing for me. I was still wearing pretty rough clothes and shoes, but I could buy new stuff right there. After a fashion, I had the money. I had skirts and stuff and sweaters; I had made my shirts.

The rest of the population in town thought it was bad. The consensus of every white European who lived outside of there was that it was all niggers and Jews. I remember in Pine County, there was a neighbor of ours named Mrs. Irvine, who told my grandmother Allen that nobody lives on Olson Memorial Highway except niggers and Jews! She was just saying it familiar because Grandma Allen was a white woman, but can you imagine some old fool saying that to her? I think Grandma wanted to hit her with her cane!

You'd see a blond-headed little kid in town here, going along talking about niggers and kikes! The blond kids who were not Jewish talk like that all the time—*nigger* would just roll out of their mouth. I didn't hear it every day, but more than I wanted to. It was kind of like today. You don't hear it, but you know it's just below the surface.

It took me until I was twenty to understand the meaning of all that—*shine, bootblack,* all the bad names, I learned them up here. I had just learned the idea early on at home that any discrimination was a lack of being human. There were people in the country who were racist, as I told you, and used the word *nigger* all the time, but they never had all the names they called us in the city.

I think if I'd grown up being called nigger, I'd have been in a fight every day. I think I would have been a little more hateful, but I would have eventually learned the right way. My father wouldn't like to mix up personal grudges with a political or economic thing—what you were working for was so much more important than the names they would call you. I was bad enough, fighting, so I'd hate to think what I would have developed into if I'd heard the word *nigger* all the time.

I remember walking with my aunt back from the flophouse joint she was a maid at. I was talking about getting a sandwich and a Coke at the downtown Woolworth and she said, "You don't have any idea, do you? I don't know if you can get anything in there." I wanted a cold drink—I was never one for a Coke, but it was hot, so I was just going to step into Woolworth's and get it. This will tell you what it was like growing up for me in the countryside—I was so used to getting what I wanted and just going about my business.

We had stores in our little towns from one end to the other, and

I could just step into a store and buy cream soda, ice cream, whatever. In the big city, you could walk in, but not get served; in the city, there were many more people that I guess grew up not knowing you. In our small towns, it was hard to be exclusionary to one family.

Many years later, when those children who sat in the lunch counters in Woolworth's, Kresge's for civil rights in the early sixties, they did it with our strong moral support, because of things like what happened when I first came to Minneapolis in 1923.

> The first summer I was here, I would see a lot of black kids out on the street along Olson Highway, standing in diapers with their bellies hanging out. They were malnourished. I was so busy thinking about school that I couldn't think about that a lot, but it affected me.
>
> And the people there who weren't working full-time, like their white neighbors were, I wondered about that. It was a rude awakening when I delved into the employment field myself. I'll never forget the feeling you get when you don't have a prayer of getting some job. You don't really feel so hurt you want to sit down and cry. What you want to do is double up your fist and start going after somebody. Pound some intelligence into their heads. That's how my reaction to it went, anyway. (CP)

But as I said, living with my aunt and uncle in north Minneapolis was not too bad a change—I was definitely used to working. I cleaned the house. I wasn't the best cook, but I made the bread. Aunt Della had a job at the old Maryland Hotel on LaSalle. I went to help her do maid work one day a week. It was an apartment hotel, with small apartments, kitchenettes. I would wash dishes, especially kitchen areas, for my aunt.

My social life wasn't much. I was quite a skiier and skater yet, and at Sumner Field, they had a court to play tennis. I was never a good tennis player, but got my exercise. And at Sumner Field, we also sledded.

I went to dances once in a blue moon, at one old place I remember, the Kissler Building, named after a Jewish doctor who owned the place, on Sixth and Lyndale Avenue North. I was always chaperoned—

I made my youngest uncle, Roscoe, take me. The black Elks would put on a dance every Monday. I met a few boys there, and I knew most of the folks were sons of women friends of my aunt, mostly railroad people that my uncle worked with. At that time, I was getting my—what do I want to say?—my initiation to jazz music, but I like the old-fashioned one-step and two-step waltzes more. Later, I came around a little bit on jazz, but still don't care much for it. That's why I'm not a bebop and rock fan. They incorporate jazz into these new-fangled styles. I guess that's how old I am; jazz sounded too modern for me.

I remember one time, I went to a dance and stayed out late, past nine. The next morning I could hardly get myself out of bed. That wasn't like me. I was home at nine the next time, I was so tired from that one little episode. Even with barn dances back home, I would come home early to get some sleep. I always did like to sleep, to the point that my body felt rested.

Anyway, the atmosphere at these dances was very good, there were mostly church people, mostly going on to higher education.

I had my first boyfriend around eighteen. He happened to be a friend of my aunt's. He was part of the Jackson family. He was nice enough, but didn't have too much sense from where I stood. He was fairly nice looking, but he didn't know politics or organizing, which was kind of hard on me. People like that, who were just climbing the ladder, didn't make much sense to me. I was able to keep him at arm's length. I never got too hung up on a good-looking man.

My aunt Della was kind of like that, too, looking to climb. My aunt had to go to the established social church in south Minneapolis. She kept asking me if I wanted to go to St. Peter's. I said no, those girls there are only looking for boyfriends. At that time, I wasn't into boyfriends. But I loved to talk politics with boys or girls.

As for the schooling I came down here for, I was taking extension courses, the equivalent of GED work, at the University of Minnesota. I didn't have any trouble getting into extension school because my grades were good. They didn't discriminate against me because of being from the country—lots of people were in those days. And it was obvious how much I knew about politics at my age.

The extension classes weren't very much—they were night classes, and that was a little better. It fit what I wanted to do better, and fit the families I worked for when I first came down here. I wanted to go to North High, but they had a tuition fee then, and it was pretty steep. My aunt didn't want to pay that.

I started at the agriculture school, and I just couldn't stand the students over there! They believed every cliché about what people believed about students of color, which would boil down to racism. I was too big and hard-looking, so they didn't say it to my face, but their body language said it all.

For example, on certain questions, teachers would ask for comments and when I raised my hand, I got looks from some students like, What the hell do you know? These were students who had never missed a meal in their lives, who didn't know what a student of color was like. Some of the teachers were shook up, too.

I don't think I encountered such racism in Lakeville or Pine City because people just didn't think of being racist in their own city—but they could be racist in the *big* city.

Look, the people I grew up around in Lakeville and Pine City were fairly intellectual people. They had a flair for very intellectual relations— they were all church people who believed just do unto others as others would do unto you. In those communities, if families were hungry, we saw to it that they were fed, no matter what race they were. If there was a new baby, everyone would flutter and do things for the baby and the mother, no matter what race they were. The only conclusion I could come to is that a little religion—of the right sort—is a good thing.

It was better then because I think there was more good Christian mentality as a way of life than there is now. Those families all talked the same, the mothers all swapped the same recipes, everyone put their feet under the same table. They certainly didn't think about it as being political. The basic thought was that it was Christian, the right thing to do.

So I went to the Minneapolis campus to do social science and political science. The whole U, it seemed like I was going off to another place when I went there. I learned in one of those old red brick buildings, over by Northrop Auditorium.

The situation was better because the students were there to study the same thing as you were. That wasn't the same for me on the ag campus. There was a lot of farm studies over there, but I had been there to study chemistry to become a pharmacist. That was my original plan. I wanted to be a pharmacist, because I had been introduced by my parents on how you test milk for sanitation. But when I went on to political science, I said what are ag people without political science?

My father thought farmers were very shortsighted in their education, because the politics of food, the price you were paid, the economic forces, were so important. So it was easy for me to give up my first dream, because I saw where I could go real easily—I could go far in politics. I thought the ag department would help me work for the quality of food and medicine, but politics would, too. I guess I was headed that way, but those ag campus people gave me a push.

I don't think a lot of minority students realize how interrelated they are—if they don't have a really complete equal opportunity, then maybe they should get involved with politics.

I always did well in class, and studying social science worked out fine. I knew more at eighteen about politics than most people ever will. I was still a teenager and I had two of the most renowned teachers in the state, Mills and Ziebarth. Everybody called him Easy Ziebarth—his initials were E. Z. They were two top-notch professors, and they did extension classes. They were played up as two of the greatest in the field of politics.

The campus life then felt kind of in between quiet and rambunctious to me. There were all these political parties there: the Young Communist League, the Young Republicans, the Young Democrats. There might have even been a Young Farmer-Labor Party, but I don't remember it. Anyway, it wasn't wild in the physical sense, but in the mental sense.

The young parties, they had assembly halls. We knew where these gatherings would be. There was some noise, and a little bit of yelling between groups, especially when we got to the time of Farmer-Laborites and Democrats, when they started trying to get the two together. There was not too much back-and-forth between Republicans and Communists because the Republicans were afraid some of that radicalism might rub off.

There were a couple of other black people on the campus that I used to sit around with. I was on the campus when they still were building Coffman Union. The minute they got the bowling alley finished there, me and another gal would bowl there at least once a week, maybe sometimes twice.

Whatever musical event they put on at Northrop Auditorium that I could afford, I'd go. I heard the Minneapolis Orchestra there for the first time. Paul Robeson, they'd hardly let him come to town without me hearing him sing. When I got to be part of the labor movement, I'd often go to cookies and coffee after his performance at some faculty member's house. It was because I was black and into labor, and so was he.

I remember hearing him talk about the great things happening in the Soviet Union—about people eating and having places to sleep, and entering the hallowed halls of medicine. I believed him because I read the press, and even though the press was anti-Soviet, once in a while they'd make a slip and write about the great advances. I don't think it was the Luce publications—*Time, Life,* and *Fortune*—[publisher Henry] Luce was very anti-Communist. I suppose it was more like if *Vogue* had decided to do a special issue on women, or there was a story in the *Ladies' Home Journal.*

I talked to Robeson quite a bit, every time I was invited to meetings, but usually some people would get him off in a corner. He was big as all outdoors, and I wasn't a withering violet either. When he sang, he'd rear back his head and poke out his chest, big as all outdoors. He was very gracious and very intellectual. He was associated with a lot of the scientists at the University of Minnesota. Within the arts and sciences it was hard to figure out who began where, but there seemed to be a lot of interplay between the faculty and labor.

One of the Oppenheimers went to school here, Frank, and I ran with him a bit. I rode with him in a wild roadster because we had to get to some DFL gathering quickly. It was convenient to get to St. Paul and burn up some gas. He was a pretty nice guy. I'd love to listen to his politics, which were DFL and radical. He talked of people having enough to eat.

Did you ever hear of a Dr. Near? He was in the rocket program and died a year or two ago. He was one of the people very involved in university political life. I know that one night, he had us over and put us all in a large living room and dining room. He put chairs out—this was a social event for Paul Robeson. I took my youngest sister, Almeda, who couldn't care less. That bothered me, because she had a very down-to-earth service job. I thought she'd be interested in it—and we had the same father—but I don't think she paid a whole lot of attention to him. For me, those meetings were interesting, those equity things for people, and how to get it.

1923: The University

Nellie settles into a seat near the rear
of the room and wraps herself in the wool coat
her mother gave her for the trip to the city,
far from the cows waiting to be milked
and the winter trap line deep in the frozen marsh.

She is eighteen,
a woman whose face stays with
the young men who slip by her as they make for
their places in the class, a colored girl whose large eyes
look through them, her heart already won
by the ideas that rush through the too-warm room
above the great river.

The lecture tonight provides a moment's rest,
and she closes those dark eyes and drifts almost into sleep.
She has already joined the Young Communists League,
the Young Socialists, then the Socialist Workers Party.
She is organizing everyone, talking to who will listen
about jobs, about food and housing for the poor,
the immigrants flooding again into the cities,
her speeches foretelling the collapse still six years in the future.
When she speaks, the color rises in her young face
and the passion makes them stop and listen.

And they are watching her too. A dark-skinned boy
Who comes to every meeting returns to his room
late at night and writes it all down,
mails in his report each week
to the Bureau's district office in Chicago—
the radical section—doing his duty, keeping America safe, from Nellie.

From "Nellie at Ninety"
(Robert L. Carothers, 1995)

Chapter 8

Young Organizer

I was in and out of the U quite a bit, all the time I was there. I was damn near twenty by the time I got that diploma, around 1925. It might sound like I was dumb, but I studied as well as worked throughout that time.

I never went to the U as an undergraduate because I went off to work. I needed money and time—two big factors in getting an education. I didn't go into college because I was getting into labor policy. I did a pretty good job with that. I was teaching where a lot of families needed one-on-one teaching on politics, a union organizing sort of thing.

I feel I have a very good education—not the structured thing, but the unstructured one that I got an honorary degree for from the state college system, on May 26, 1995.

You ask me whether I'm a hypocrite for pushing education so hard but not going for a college degree. I would say that there's not necessarily a contradiction—the intelligent get an education, but it is not necessarily a degree. I've never seen so many degreed fools as I've seen in my life in the last ten years.

> At that great institution, the University of Minnesota, I found out only too well what dad meant by *educated fool*—someone who can remember everything they read in a book, but can't analyze what they read or live by what they claim to believe in. (CP)

To me, here's what education is: I remember reading all these words when I was a kid, and sometimes they didn't make sense. But I kept at it, and as I did, the door of my mind opened up, and that gives a person so much freedom to know what's going on around them, without having to struggle so hard to learn it by experience. It's opening a great big door to other learning. You need access to quality teachers, yes, and to quality institutions, but I guess I never thought the actual degree was so important, really, as long as you are pursuing understanding and making yourself more aware of why things are.

That's probably based on my own experience, mixing work and school—I guess what they call continuing education now. I was just ahead of my time. I was probably at the U twice a month, once a week, going to these seminars, taking classes, going to visit professors. Lots of us did that. We did get college credits.

I figured it out once. I've spent forty-one years, not really in school, not in the sense of a structured program, but going back and forth, to conferences, classes, seminars, that sort of thing, studying what labor and politics are all about. I figured in the years I went to ag school in that.

I had a lot of classes and causes. I stayed at MIT once—they had this conference on restructuring public education, and I spent ten days involved in the studies, getting together with various experts, in 1995. A lot of people said, isn't it interesting that this ninety-year-old woman is in class at her age. I got knocked down a lot of times too—a lot of people didn't understand how important minority participation was. I would have fights with people in those conferences, over grassroots people being trained in politics. I want to bring the rank and file into policy making, but for some others, there was a little bit of the elitist side, that only high officials could do that.

I remember once, when they opened up Metro State University in 1972, they tried to get me in as a student, to serve as an example. They had raised the money, which was part of why they contacted me to be a student. I didn't want to do it because I was still working in my own business. I was busy all the time then, with my alteration business, and with Democratic national politics.

At the University, Nellie met a man who would ignite many of her later accomplishments. Never a central figure himself, Swan Assarson is woven into the profiles of many Minneapolis labor figures. According to the radical labor historian Carl Ross, Assarson arrived in America a "somewhat itinerant organizer intending to build a Swedish worker's society."

Even though I never graduated, the Minneapolis campus was where most of my education came about, and a lot of it wasn't in the classroom. One person was responsible for a lot. He came from Sweden, and he was an old-time socialist named Swan Assarson.

I met Swan in the late twenties, right around the start of the Great Depression, I think. He was somewhere around fifty to sixty, one of these older men who hung around the U, around Coffman, and I expect even around the student union before Coffman. He had his faculties together.

He reminded me philosophically of my father, but that ended there because Swan was such a small man. I'm trying to think of a reasonable facsimile; he was the size of Jimmy Cagney, but not that boisterous. I would say he was five-five, five-six, and he was beginning to get a little stomach, sort of chesty.

He would kind of wander around, whenever he'd see four or five students in comfortable chairs, all he had to do was hear them discussing something interesting, he'd ask if he could join the group. Today, I suppose, especially if women were present, they'd be thinking about harassment. I knew the group I would talk heavy politics with and never thought much strange about guys like him. A few professors would hobnob around, and Swan should've been a professor in some high Ivy League college, because he had politics way before them. He wasn't a teacher, but apparently his own history, his own background, his basic intelligence, he had it all together to grasp things like the basic equality of man. But being that much of a socialist probably didn't help him then in academia. You know what Sweden was in those days—very socialist.

From everything I could see, he was a hanger-on of students, to make sure they got the proper education around organizing. He read everything that was printed.

Swan was great people. He was kind of a rough old guy, but to me he was a great person. The thing I liked about him is that he was so down to earth, and he saw good in all people. I found him very astute in the total academics—there were very few people could hold a candle to his world knowledge. He had lived it, in Europe and over here. When he started telling me about a lot of the world history he was involved in, I thought, this was someone I could trust. I am such a history nut. I don't want to hear any music I don't know the history of, I don't want to see a Shakespeare play that I don't know the whole history of. If there's an odd animal out there, I'm part of it.

Two issues that I heard him talk about were issues that I had thought about my entire life. The right of labor to organize and the right of black people to live and not be hung from a hanging tree. Swan talked about blacks being equal—which was certainly not the way most people spoke of blacks at that time. When the subject got to Native Americans, he just went into a tizzy about how they were treated. That really impressed me. There was never a racist bone in his body. Swan was very influential on my life, and he pushed me to really get involved in the Young Communists.

I was attracted to the Young Communists. They had the best programs on education and training for labor—they went way beyond anybody else. They talked sense. To me, it was like taking about the Civil War, after it was declared over. I could never understand why people felt they knew what the Civil War was when they thought only about Lincoln freeing the black slaves, then never thought of Northern industrial slaves. I've always thought that was one of the biggest holes in history. The Young Communists talked about the oppression of all people, and pushed hard to educate and organize to stop it.

They got members by furthering education, why people should vote, why people should further certain political issues, like what you would do in any left-wing party. They believed in doing good educational work, and didn't just talk about it. And they believed whole-heartedly in better education for everybody. The Young Communist League had educated people, and thought that this was the right way to be.

I was pretty active for a couple of years or so. I just had a lot of other things to do, thought I'd learned from them what I could, especially about organizing. I set about putting those efforts into the unions and the NAACP.

In 1924, when I was nineteen, my aunt—the one who did maid work—had a friend who had a job at the Minneapolis Athletic Club. They kept me out of there at first after I applied—I was a lady-in-waiting. But it wasn't that long before a job as an elevator operator came open.

I remember that when I finally got an interview, I had to write something about myself. I just wrote about my age and a few things I had done on the farm. I had been a pretty good mechanic—not to the extent of taking an elevator apart, but I think that experience helped. I had to take an exam from a city engineer about elevator operation—nothing too big, just remembering what to do if anything went wrong. It was pretty obvious I could do that.

The Athletic Club looked kind of plush to me—not too plush, but beyond what most people had. Most of the males in my family were railroad people, and they lived pretty good. They had enough to eat, a piano in the living room, good furniture, rugs. So it wasn't as big a change as you'd think. The Athletic Club was glamorous up to a point. But I was a practical person, and that sort of took the glamour edge off. I never got carried away with the big oriental rugs, or the grand piano in the lobby. Just about any owner of any corporate-type business was eligible for membership, and there were some politicians.

My favorite was a Republican senator, a federal judge later appointed by Hubert, Luther Youngdahl. I remember him because he was nice, decent people, who didn't look at you like he was going to step on you like some of the others did. Sometimes the look said a lot.

If you were a woman, they did try to feel around you—a lot of that went on. They knew which girls to put their hands on. They would try to be nice to you, but they looked at me like I was some kind of animal. I remember one man—I'll call him a gentleman in honor of his passing—who I overheard one day asking someone, "Aren't there any nice girls I can take out on a date?" When someone mentioned my name, he exclaimed, "You mean that wild Indian from northern Minnesota?!" I thought, Good enough, you old fuddy-duddy.

A lot of times, for these men, it didn't make any difference if they took out the black checkout girls or the white women in the dining room—they would walk down the streets with anybody if they felt attached. I call it the freedom of the well-heeled. And part of it was that they felt they could do anything to a woman. The Athletic Club was often a den of animalism. Women didn't count. Those things also shaped your beliefs, where you came from. I remember one day running the elevators. There was an old fool, he'd just gotten married to this good-looking woman—well, we all knew she had been a prostitute. Someone else on the elevator, another member, said something to him about a black worker he had hired. This person asked the man, "How much did you get her for?" Can you believe that? "How much did you get her for?" And he said, "I pay her less—these people don't know any better." And I just sat there thinking, You old fool, I *do* know better.

They treat you like you are way below them, that you don't know what they know. They treat you like an animal with no understanding. People keep asking why people of color hate the other part of the larger community. Well, these little black kids running around hungry and dirty have an intellect that people don't give them credit for. And that just fuels the anger.

Floyd B. Olson, who I think was Hennepin County Attorney at the time, was a member of the Athletic Club. He later became a great Farmer-Labor governor. His aide, a man by the name of Ed McMahon, had a room at the club.

I don't know how wealthy Olson was, but he didn't want for anything. Carl Coleman was a parking lot owner in town, and Olson could park anywhere in town without paying at a Coleman lot. They were Olson's rear guard. He and his cronies would go up to McMahon's room on the ninth floor at the club every day at four o'clock and stay there all night. They'd make one call to the checker to order whiskey—I was not on the front desk then.

It was not hard to know what they were doing—there were calls constantly coming for whiskey, tables of food. Women weren't supposed to be in the club, and we who worked there would just dash in and out of their room when we had to deliver something. We were not supposed to know what was going on. Sometimes, there were women in there we were not supposed to know about, but like the CIA, we knew but made no comment.

The members would make a beeline for my elevator, which was closest to a corner. They'd go into a hallway and open a back door for the woman, then take the freight elevator up with the girl.

They were oftentimes doing hard political business, he and his cronies up there. There was a lot of socializing, too—who wouldn't want to hang on to a Hennepin County Attorney or a future governor? The Hennepin County Attorney was practically next to the governor in dollars they could spend—still is.

I think I worked at the Athletic Club twenty-six years over two periods. What got me fired from the Athletic Club the first time, in the late twenties, was labor activities—everybody knew that. The manager at the time, McClure, he was an old railroad executive who had gotten burned because the railroads were tough on unions, and by the twenties, employers were having it very rough. The unions had started getting what they wanted in contracts.

The assistant manager, Fred Andrews, he too was a railroad man who had run up against the dining car waiters. They fired me for what they officially called insubordination—I had raised hell with the manager, something about shifting time around. But part of it, too, was that they said I was pressuring people working there. I don't know how valid that was. I've never run into anyone before or since who said I was bothering people to be in the union.

The way they did it, the assistant manager called me into his office. He was a very stupid kind of man in my estimation. No public relations to him at all—he just blurted out what he felt his boss would say. He said, "You're trying to do that union organizing around here." The Wagner Labor Relations Act, which protected union organizers, came later, under Roosevelt.

All of us who worked on behalf of unions stood a chance to lose jobs, to get blackballed. I didn't *want* to be hungry, lack a roof over my head. But I guess I did pretty good. I wasn't worried about finding a job, or having enough to eat. When it looked like things were falling down, I'd just go to the farm and get a hundred-pound sack of potatoes and onions. My father made sure we never ran out of potatoes!

But my first time talking union at the Athletic Club, that's really all I was doing—talking it around. I wasn't really organizing, but I did have an opinion. It was over quickly, though, and I was out of there.

I went to the old West Hotel for five, six, seven years in the late twenties, early thirties. I didn't take a pay cut, I got a ten-dollar-a-month increase. The West was a very old hotel, and the owner had a suite of rooms there for herself, her secretary, and her secretary's secretary, plus a half dozen Chihuahuas. There was nice upholstery in these old hotels, good old oak and mahogany. There were a few families, who had like hot plates, but ate out most of the time. Traveling salespeople, coming and going for fifty years.

I talked with one person about unions there. She worked with me on my shift, and her husband was in the Brotherhood of Sleeping Car Porters. But I never tried to organize a union at the West. See, at the Athletic Club, among the people I wanted to help, the vision was greater—the people wanted to be organized, be real human beings. We didn't have that many types of people at the West. I did have some intelligence to know what I was up against, and didn't want to put my head all the way into the stove. There were strong human relations among the employees at the Athletic Club, much stronger.

I stayed at the West until the new owners took over and didn't want any black people. That was the first experience I had with being cost a job because I was black. There were people in the elevator engineering operation who were not fired. I don't remember any whites who were fired.

I was shocked when I got fired at West. I thought it was about the most inhumane thing they could do, since people needed jobs. They said they were making changes, reorganization changes. That sounds like jargon now when you want to put ten to fifteen thousand people out of work, regardless of race, creed, or color. For the most part, they replaced us with white elevator operators, and they were men.

It was a racist policy, and there wasn't much we could do. The only black people they kept around were the shoeshine people. I don't remember the exact date; folks think you remember everything in detail, but the dates do get hazy sometimes.

It wasn't very long before the Athletic Club hired me back. This was 1933. I still kept in touch with people at the Athletic Club, talking up a union—I would always say we've got to tighten the union up— and one day, one of the girls said to see the manager that hired me originally. I saw the department manager and his manager. They hired me back because they got a couple of younger members on the board who were not thinking like their fathers were. They believed unions were a respectable business. Or a necessary evil. I don't know how it went down, never did get full picture of that.

Two young men on the board apparently talked about it at a board meeting. I don't mind throwing names out, but I can't remember them right now. I do recall one young man, he belonged to a family grocery business, and he was very helpful. I think the reason was that his truck drivers were already organized, and he knew enough about how that had worked to know unions weren't evil and could be good.

There was another, older man, who had a wholesale business. He was very active in his church, an Episcopalian who lived in Lowry Hill. This person may have been a turning point, because of his Christianity. I understand that through his church, they tried to bring in black people for jobs at the Athletic Club. The only thing I can halfway remember is that he was somewhat in the wholesale business, like the grocery business, too. I'm so nosy I'm surprised I slipped up on that.

So I was hired back as an elevator operator, though I had to do a few weeks in the checkroom. Nobody in management said anything to me when I went back. I knew all the women there very well; as a group they were very close. They certainly hurried up to be a part of the union.

I woke up one morning and found myself an organizer, there in 1934. What happened to set it all off is that one day the Athletic Club told us they had to cut our pay. This was the depression, and they cut us from fifteen dollars a week down to twelve-fifty. That sent me right up the wall because that two-fifty paid for groceries—and not the meat, but the milk and the bread. I knew because I ran a bill at the grocery store.

What they told us was they couldn't afford us. I knew differently. You pretty much knew what the club's income was—they put out the final statistics, not for me to see, but some members had 'em.

And believe me, I went out and got 'em from anyplace and anybody I could. The best place was from the women who worked in the office. The management didn't realize this, but the office women were interested in a union, too, because they wanted an increase in pay, and they wanted to help whoever was going to do the work. They just gave me the statistics, the club financial reports, so we knew everything about how they were doing, which was just fine.

When a few of us said, it's time for a union, we didn't know too much about where to go for help. But we had some people deliver to the freight elevator operators, and they had contacts with the Teamsters. The first thing they said was, "Nellie, you've got to have handpicked people, and these people should get to know the restaurant workers." We became known as Local 665.

The union people talked to me about the foundation of labor unions, and it wasn't much different from the farm movement I'd been involved in my whole life. George Naumoff, a man I worked with, and I talked to the workers every chance we got.

He was on the freight elevator, just inside the door. He was Croat, as he called himself. He was a good-looking man, five-ten, five-eleven, and dark curly hair—great big curls on his head, two or three inches, and he would comb it back. He was a very decent person. He had an accent, but he got to a place where he could make people understand what he was about.

George was a union guy, in terms of economics and education. I think it was his background. Every Yugoslav I met, even before Tito took over, was well educated, and had a halfway flair for a socialistic way of doing politics, the way the Swedes and Norwegians did it. They were notorious for hard-nosed labor beliefs.

George was so important because the trick at the Athletic Club was that employees could ride the freight elevators, but management, of course, almost never did. So anytime someone got in one of those, George would give them a good talking to, or they would ride the employee elevator and I'd get 'em.

> People were at my mercy because the employees' dressing rooms were on the 14th floor. We'd strong-arm them into joining the union before we'd let them off the elevator. (MWP)

I had a few of 'em just jump straight up and down—they didn't want to hear anything about a union! I guess the prejudices came from their parents. I, of course, had made it a point to learn everything about labor in this country. I had the advantage of my father being an organizer. I was such a hard-nosed person that I'd always done what I wanted.

George and I both worked on authorization cards. Authorization means that you want to join the union, or you don't, because you have a yes or no vote. Signing the card means you would join the union, but it was much wider than that. The whole syndrome means not only joining the organization, but working for it—in your communication with people, and on what the program and the contract should be. You agree to be a member of the union, and working to get the organization organized.

It was very vicious organizing unions at that time. A lot of people were beaten up and killed for organizing unions. The business community would hire strikebreakers to do just that, especially in the industrial unions, the Teamsters and the like.

I watched some of the stuff, the violence with the Teamsters' strike in 1934, because I wanted to know the full philosophy around strikebreakers. I did see some fistfights and that sort of thing, people knocked down, who were working for the Teamsters down in the old warehouse district, which was really the market district. The people in the market business, they had their nameplates over their walls where folks would drive the truck or team of horses. There was one row after another. Now, of course, they are all trucks, but at the time I came to Minneapolis, it was a combination of trucks and horses.

Sometimes, I had to go through town, I had a little roadster—well, not really a roadster, but a little Chev with a rumble seat in it. My sister Gladys, every year, she was having a new baby, and it seemed like my duty was to get those kids and her around, so I was always around the market. I wanted to see what was going on and I was curious, and I wanted to see what I was supporting.

The strike went on for quite a while. It depended on the time of day. Sometimes four or five people would group off, and maybe only two would be fighting, but there would be a grouping around them.

It would be whoever the power structure hired to break up the strike, to go after people picketing. The Teamsters, the truck drivers in the marketplace, were picketing all over the place.

I was going home every weekend and wanted to talk to the folks about what was going on. It made me careful about what I was saying at work to people in the power structure.

My father could've been designated by the power structure as a picketer and beaten up because he was bringing potatoes and rutabagas to the soup kitchen, what they called where the Teamsters were fed, at Centennial Place on Chicago Avenue. My father was a pretty sharp politician. He read what was up, and would not drive willy-nilly into the area, the territory where strikebreakers were watching. He just kept a low profile.

I do know the anti-Teamster feeling was rampant and wicked, especially at the clubs and hotel. The members were talking about those thugs, whatever bad thing they could say. Look, I see the corporate world—I know people in recent years who are not part of the labor movement bought that jargon, that the corporate people were the good people, but they were as antihuman as you could be then.

It could've happened—I could've gotten beaten up. I didn't, though. I always had a very good, very sharp notion of exactly what could happen. Basically, though, I never got beaten up because I was a woman.

You would think someone would tip off management at the Athletic Club and they would at least give me a good talking-to, and that's exactly what happened—but within the bailiwick of Captain Crowder. He was the boss, and yes, he was black. He was the captain of the elevator operators, the checkroom, the bellmen, the janitors.

He was a good man, but he was old-fashioned—he had a work ethic second to none. Maybe it's because of that work ethic that I think of him sometimes as a father type of man. For all the upbraiding he'd do, Captain Crowder knew I was a good worker and he could set his watch by me. I could read him like a watch, too, like some children read their parents.

What did I do? I simply ignored it and walked away. He would say, "Allen, I understand you're going to a union meeting tonight"—he'd just rock back on his heels. Then he'd say, "Anyone going to a union meeting is out of a job!" Then the next day, he'd say, "Allen, I heard you went to a union meeting—and the next time you do it you're definitely out of a job!"

I don't think he did anything because the Brotherhood of Sleeping Car Porters was getting pretty strong. I had four uncles in the Brotherhood and word got back to Captain Crowder not to be too rough. He knew the background of the people who worked for him.

It helped so much that unions stuck together, and I'd like to think I perpetuated that when I belonged to a union educational group that included the Brotherhood of Sleeping Car Porters. It was called the A. Philip Randolph Institute, a spin-off of the Brotherhood designed to educate people about labor, named after their great leader, a local man.

Though the Brotherhood did not provide explicit help, my uncles and I discussed a lot of things, the verbiage of what we were advocating for, the economics. To get to the economics, all I had to do was think of my father, spreading word about Non-Partisan League. My vision, because of my father, well, the politics were already indelibly in my mind. The only difference with the farmers was that we were rank-and-file employees of someone else's business.

My uncles pretty much did what all good rank-and-file union members did. Number one, they fought for the right to organize wherever they worked, and on how much they'd earn, and what else to get into the contract. They never held office, and they were unpaid for this. The uncles were Walter, my father's oldest brother; Clem out of St. Louis was the third brother down the pecking line; Clarence, the one I lived with in Minneapolis; then the youngest, Roscoe, who lived with us on the farm in Pine County and then with Clarence.

Clarence was the biggest talker, the smartest of the whole outfit, but people didn't pay attention to him. The one that A. Philip Randolph called the Minnesota connection was Walter. There's a difference in the black community that the so-called white community, or the liberal community, does not understand: Walter was a churchman, strong in the community on feeding people, getting people jobs and that sort of thing. All of those very basic things. It made a bigger difference what you did than what you said to most people then.

Uncle Walter would turn over in his grave if I called him a radical—he was low-key even as he's convincing you to put your head on the stove! But he would just keep on saying that it was the right thing to join the union, and to participate in the union. If you think about it, that was pretty radical in those days. I always admired him because he got things done.

Roscoe was pretty much like Clarence. He talked a lot, which was good for spreading the word about the organization. Clem was kind of halfway between the radical guys and Walter. He married a woman who was a teacher.

I don't think any of my uncles experienced any violence toward them because of union activities. What I said about Walter paving the way, well, they all went to church in their own fashion. Their mother belonged to Zion Baptist Church, on Eleventh and Lyndale; it had been a synagogue. There wasn't much union beating here in Minneapolis toward blacks. All of us were at the end of a gun organizing, but we were decent people, we raised a good family.

The people that really got beat up were the white people in the union, the engineers on the trains and the folks shoveling coke. The difference was the attitude of some of the people. I think the folks who did the beatings considered blacks more religious and Christian, which they were. Of course, they weren't treated better when it came to jobs and other things. That was pretty interesting. I do know what I saw around me—that black people were considered much more Christian than average working whites at the time.

The Brotherhood printed and talked about the social structure of economics, but Captain Crowder was almost an intellectual doormat for the white power structure.

When it came to the union, I think what Captain Crowder was most afraid of was being written up in the black paper—it wasn't the *Minneapolis Spokesman* yet. They could write about the black captain who helped get all these people with good jobs at the Athletic Club fired for organizing, with their brothers in unions.

The owner of the paper was a union member, and was very dedicated to trade unionism. This was Cecil Newman, of the Brotherhood of Sleeping Car Porters. He served on just about every community committee he had time for. The Urban League board, the NAACP board, and the business community boards that wanted him to legitimize them. He knew what was going on in the community, and you did, too. Not everyone read the *Spokesman,* but that didn't matter. For example, a couple of us at the Athletic Club would pick up a copy and talk about it in the dressing room, and pretty soon everyone in that dressing room would be repeating it as if they read it themselves.

It was the number one paper for a number of years. There was the *Observer,* the *Twin Cities Courier,* owned by the Kyle family. But nothing ever since 1933–34 was equal to the *Spokesman* in bringing the real story to the people. Like now, a lot of people go through the motions, like KMOJ radio—a lot of people flex their vocal muscles and don't know what's going on.

Newman and the *Daily Freiheit,* the Jewish paper, they traded news all the time. When we got the campaign going to support Hubert Humphrey, one of my mentors was Frank Boyd from the Brotherhood of Sleeping Car Porters in St. Paul, and Mr. Newman, Rubin Latz, and Mike Finklestein from the Ladies Garment Union. These were my labor mentors—blacks and Jews.

> [Reuben and Frank] would go to political meetings and all but tear each other apart and then they'd go out and have coffee together. I said, boy, there's so much knowledge in these two people! So I just almost absorbed every word they said.
>
> I remember that Frank Boyd was a deacon in Pilgrim Baptist Church in St. Paul and they put him off the deacon's board because of his union activities. So he sat in church and somebody made a re-mark to him that he wasn't supposed to be there. He said, "You have the right to put me off the deacon's board but you can't put me out of church 'cause me and God's going to sit here every Sunday morning." And that's the way he was, you know. [He] defied everything for what he believed was right. (MHS, 6–7)

North Minneapolis had a lot of Jewish people and a strong labor group. We ran into a lot of conservative business owners that did not employ blacks. But the B'nai B'rith took the community on about racism, and Hadassah, their women's group, was very big on equality.

The only religious advocate for union people at the time was the Beth El Synagogue in north Minneapolis. A lot of gals there were my friends. There were labor-friendly lawyers like Latz and Finklestein.

There was a Labor Lyceum, which is what they called the Jewish labor assembly. This gal—her father was a salesperson for bedspreads—she heard we were struggling to organize a union, so she said come to the synagogue. We went to the synagogue and the rabbi said, "We are supporting labor at every turn. If a union is starting, we will help it grow. And if it's not, we should start one!" Boy, those were good, powerful words. I wished churches would have said things like that.

I am surprised at how little of a role churches played. I remember only too well the churches that were antilabor in the twenties and thirties. They tried to say that the labor movement was not Christian, that it was atheistic, that it came from the Communists. Those churches that were well heeled and supported by the power structure were very antilabor, and that played a big role in the Teamster's strike of 1934. There were such things as propagandizing by leafleting outside the church, and within the newsletter for churches. Periodically I was handed a leaflet, this was handed out at a church. The leaflets were always posing a question about the social life out there: Are unions good? Are unions locked up with the Mafia, the bad crust of society? They insinuated in a very negative way.

The red issue did seep in, but that wasn't quite what bothered me—I was raised that radicalism would be red-baited. This was just that unions were bad—they were always trying to link the unions up with racketeering.

Of course, not all labor people were Communists, and labor was doing a lot for the working man and woman—more I daresay than some of those churches that these working people belonged to! Some of the Catholic churches got beat up so bad by their own members that they eventually became pro-labor. There was a groundswell of construction workers who told them they should practice what they preached. That's where a lot of pro-life women who came into the labor movement, by the way, and that caused problems later on when abortion became a big split in the DFL party. If people wonder why I'm not as harsh on pro-lifers as some of the feminists, it's because I can remember us all coming together back in those days. That's not to say I'm pro-life, though.

We were doing well because we talked housing, we talked bread and butter, we talked health. We were upset when we heard ministers were not doing that, when they thought that wasn't part of their message. We thought that we had the most Christian part of His message.

My mentors taught me how they brought in the whole question of the fight for equality within the labor movement—that we didn't have to be a one-issue movement. I never called Rubin Latz anything other than Mr. Latz. He was such a man of intellect and humanity. He realized there was a big agenda. Instead of just going for more money, go for equal rights for all people—that other people's privilege is yours, too. Get some of that for them and you increase it for yourself. You realize it's just not me fighting for myself. It affects other people of any nationality. And it made the coalition that would support us stronger.

The difference between the first and second time organizing the Athletic Club was nothing that strange and hard to understand. It was a difference in political timing. The first time, labor didn't scare them quite as much, but the second time it did, or vice versa.

There were different stages about the political acceptance of labor. The corporate world, the power structure looked around and saw the Farmer-Labor Party taking one office after another. That played a role in helping us organize, that there was a politic group of people supported by labor.

By that second time, some labor people had negotiated some pretty good contracts. After the election of Roosevelt in 1932, the big-money people said, do you realize how close we are to communism? I'm glad my parents taught me enough not to be afraid of that word, but I'm also glad some people were ignorant so that they would sit down with labor because they were so scared.

The growing threat of a tight union organization made them treat us more carefully. They had something of a grasp of PR then. We also made it clear that whites and blacks would be treated the same. It looked as though some good PR caught up with the managers—they knew the stakes were higher if they tried firing us now.

There were also some people there, as I said, who were humane. As for who convinced the bosses, besides the board members who helped me get my job back, I have an idea. The wife of one of the board members had been working on an employment project for people of color. There was a part of that crowd that would do very humane types of things—you can't believe the history that says these were all evil people. When the board got their comeuppance with our union drive, I think some of the members, including the ones who helped me get my job back, said they had to do something to guarantee the black community jobs, that it was good for the whole city.

It was impressive—we got the whole housekeeping department, the service department, and the kitchen and dining room employees. They were all in the union, with the exception of the maître d' and the top waitresses. They weren't in the section I was in, but we eventually got them into Cooks and Waiters Local 458. I was Local 665. Bartenders were in 152. Now that's all part of Local 17 of the International Hotel and Restaurant union. But we all came under supervision of the International Hotel and Restaurant union.

Captain Crowder seemed relieved when our organizing succeeded. He may have even been sympathetic to the cause. He had been through a lot—he was an older man who had traveled through the South. It was hard to find a stupid black person on the question of human treatment who had traveled around any. Most were past masters at reading their white counterparts.

He adhered to the letter of the law on the contract we negotiated. He never said anything about union matters again, and we didn't make him pay for yelling at us. We even raised his wages in the contract, and he got another week's vacation! We wrote it right into the first contract!

All through my time at the Athletic Club, I never stopped organizing— I was still doing the elevator operator position. Then I went beyond that to become a receptionist, an elevator starter, which was supposed to be a cut above an elevator operator. Really several steps above—two or three thousand dollars' worth.

Elevator starters stood outside and counted people, from eleven o'clock to two, when the club did a tremendous business for lunch. All these elevators could carry twenty-five hundred pounds. I was very good at gauging weight, sizing up people, hauling around all that wood and hay when I was younger. I would make sure those elevators carried all the people they could, but not too many!

The club had so many meetings, the Real Estate Board, the three big service organizations such as the Rotarians, the higher education groups—groups like that. But we had some different kinds. During the forties, the First Baptist Church with Dr. Richard Raines of the America First movement, the anti-Semitic group, met there. Several of us elevator operators discussed all that, the meaning behind America First. It was me, Eva Pugh, and Louise Cain.

There was a man who was close to Louise, a member named Mr. Garber. He had a junkyard in north Minneapolis—he sold a lot of metal to the federal government. He was a nice man in many ways. He and Louise got to talking about Germany—in the thirties and forties, what was going on—and a lot of us got to talking with them. We discussed how deep the anti-Semitic feeling was among those America Firsters. He felt anti-Semitism was encroaching on the world. Some of those America Firsters would have died if they knew what went on among the three of us.

When you're talking of the anti-Semitism of Minnesota, the man who wrote the famous story in 1946 about Minneapolis being the most anti-Semitic place in the country, Carey McWilliams, a lot of his information came through me. I was the person who was the whistle blower on the Athletic Club on this. By that time, I was on the reception desk. I did research—I knew what church a member went to, what his job was, the business, everything about the background of the person, what motivates them. And if their organization was not committed to equality, I knew that, too.

Now, McWilliams wasn't meeting personally with me, but with Doug and Mary Hall, and their contingent, about how people lived. Doug Hall was one of the outstanding labor lawyers in the city. Mary later worked on Minnesota Consumer Affairs, that sort of thing. I was feeding them so they could feed him.

Doug Hall told me something was going to be in the paper, which turned out to be McWilliams's big exposé and it hit with a bang. I had seen plenty of anti-Semitism at the Athletic Club myself. Just the fact that the America Firsters met there should tell you something.

––––––––

In the autumn 1946 issue of Common Ground *magazine, the muck-raking California journalist Carey McWilliams dubbed Minneapolis the "capitol* [sic] *of anti-Semitism in the United States," scandalizing a town that fancied itself progressive and tolerant. McWilliams noted: "Years ago, a few Jews were accepted, as life members, in the Minneapolis Athletic Club. But the board of the club, contrary to a long established practice, has of recent years refused to recognize the transfer of these memberships to the sons of deceased members and has stated that it will not accept further Jewish applications." (McWilliams's article was an attempt to "account for the divergent anti-Semitic patterns to be found in . . . St. Paul and Minneapolis." Hence his title "Minneapolis: The Curious Twin.")*

––––––––

The membership of the Athletic Club had absorbed something called the Commercial Club, which was on the top floor of the Radisson. It was an all-Jewish club, because Jews could not get into the Athletic Club when the Commercial Club started.

There was a lot of financial wherewithal in the Commercial Club, which the Athletic Club needed to expand its building. Because of the grandfather clause, a lot of Jews suddenly became members automatically. That's how that junk dealer named Garber was around.

But the Athletic Club old guard tried to phase them out once they had their money. They would not approve sons and relatives as members.

I had overheard about the two sons of the Freeman family not being allowed to be members; it wasn't hard to figure out it was anti-Semitism. I heard people talk, talk to both of the brothers. I knew the treatment they were getting, how many applications they made. It didn't stop the club from taking their father's money—the sons could use their dad's number, but they couldn't be members.

The Athletic Club old guard tried to make sure they gave Commercial Club members bad treatment in the dining room. The old-time Athletic Club help, they gave them service like it didn't matter where they came from, but on stuff that management controlled, like reservations, seating at certain tables, the availability of meeting rooms, the Jews were very much second-class citizens. I personally never saw anyone from management issue an order myself. They knew better than to come near me. But you learned from what people who weren't Jews said about people who were. And with a little bit of intelligence—if I could grant that to myself—you could pretty easily put that together.

There were other Jews, like the Bernie and Leo Harris family, no one messed with them because of their wealth. Also, their name didn't sound Jewish, so it didn't get talked about much.

Occasionally they would even let blacks in to do business. There were the Gibbs brothers, five of them that were in the laundry business. They met as a part of that industry at Athletic Club—a lot of business societies met there. No one kept them out, and I never heard anything antiblack about them as far as their business there. The club members almost referred to them in a prideful way, like those were the good blacks. But you bet they had a policy against blacks becoming members. The reason I mentioned this is it's a good example of how you can just be in that casual kind of business setting, be respected within the time limits of having of do business there.

Doug Hall was a labor lawyer, which pretty much disqualified him for membership. There was nothing the management could say about Doug or even Carey McWilliams coming in, if a member was with them.

Roy Bjorklund, the official head minister of Central Lutheran Church in Minneapolis, was the caliber of person, the status of person, who would know and assist Carey McWilliams.

It's hard to figure out why humane people would be part of an anti-Semitic place. Maybe the church bought a membership like the businesses did. There might have even been church meetings there. An awful lot of Lutherans were members of the Athletic Club, and they were pretty much the power structure in town then.

I suppose my rationale with Carey McWilliams was to bring about as much support from people of the community as possible.

Chapter 9

Men and Marriage

Husbands? That's stuff that's not too important to me. My first was Clyde Stone. He was a mechanic. He mostly worked around the garage. We married in 1931, when I was twenty-six years old.

I first met Clyde at my grandmother Allen's house on Dupont Avenue North, right on the corner of Third, Fourth, one block off Glenwood. She moved to the city after my grandfather died, in the thirties.

Grandma Allen was a good friend of his mother. I thought he was a nice-looking man, and he was handy. I liked men who could do things around the house! My second husband, Lee Johnson, was a cement finisher and a good one. He did work on airstrips on Iwo Jima and Okinawa.

I don't know what sparked Clyde and me other than we just liked each other and gabbed. We both liked to go fishing, and we gabbed about that. He did not have many hobbies besides fishing. Once in a while, we'd go up to the farm and get back into the swing of farming. He was from Mt. Pleasant, Iowa, a farmer, and his mother was a teacher. It was kind of similar to my background, but he never dabbled in politics.

I liked to hunt, but he didn't know too much about that. We went pheasant hunting on the farm—they almost picked them up and brought pheasants to you, there were so many.

Clyde and I dated a long time, longer than I did with anyone else, about three years. That was long for me! Our first date was to a movie in January. Clyde got his mother's car.

One thing about dating and marrying during the depression, we didn't have much money. At that time, there was no inflation, and prices for farm products were very low. But for the most part, my family didn't hurt too much overall. We did know how bad it was because my uncle Walter fed people who lived nearby—they did that because they had jobs. My uncle, of course, worked with the railroad, and my aunt and even her mother had a full-time job.

One reason I married Clyde is that he was very much taken in by my family. I guess a little bit, yeah, was to please my family. My grandmother Allen was down my throat, morning, noon, and night, that I was twenty-six years old and not married! Not only was I not married, but I wasn't going to make a child. She was living at my uncle's when Clyde and I were dating, and she said it was *not* nice for a girl to be in her twenties and not married. And I was still in school, too.

I guess there was enough of the old-fashioned about me to respect my elders. Really, I didn't have time for a man, but my grandmother Allen was the hard-nosed talker about me getting married. I was staying with one of my uncles at the time, and it was handy for her to come down on my head periodically.

I kind of laughed at her, told her how things had changed since she was a girl. She got married at seventeen. She had Uncle Walter just before she turned eighteen. I didn't tell her much, because she had a fiery temper too. I wasn't that concerned about getting married. I just wanted to keep going to school, to work. My grandma, I would do anything for. She was a very religious woman.

There were a few things I realized when I married Clyde. I wasn't swept off my feet, but one of the things that really kind of got me going is that he was just fine with me working if I wanted to. A lot of husbands wouldn't let wives work, but I wanted to see my own paycheck. We talked about that early on and we didn't have any arguments about that. That kind of excited me.

Almost any time I wanted to go back to school, for seminars and the like, I could, and I liked that. Clyde didn't have too much choice, but we didn't argue about it to any extent. I was back in and out of school constantly, going to conferences, anything to increase my knowledge of labor and politics—I did that all the time.

We didn't go dancing a lot, but we did go out. A lot of the so-called cabarets or bars had a dancing space, an orchestra or a piano player. I liked to dance because of the exercise I got. Clyde was like me, he was fair—he stumbled over his feet from time to time.

He worked in a garage for the most part, a car polisher. It was pretty good money. He liked that.

We did go to speakeasies during Prohibition, but I was always afraid. I heard about raids, and I knew people had been thrown in jail overnight. I didn't mind being thrown in jail for my union activities, but I didn't want to go there over some speakeasy!

I wondered why they called 'em speakeasies when people were so quiet all the time. Everybody had their bottle, you got your drink under the table. I also saw a lot of having to identify yourself.

They were everyplace. There were a couple of places I attended on Olson Highway, just like clubs now. I would be there with employees from the food department at the Athletic Club, from the service department, and some employees from the club orchestra. Usually, some of the more knowing people would take you somewhere.

I remember when Prohibition lifted in 1933. Clyde and I would kind of limit ourselves to a beer on Saturday. There was quite a group of people that would go out on the weekends. You'd go out and have a draft beer, and eat a lot of pretzels.

A couple of our friends were Clarence and Helen Miller. They were kind of our age—there were four years between Clyde and me. Clarence worked for the Greyhound or Jefferson bus company, and I was trying to think what Helen did—maybe worked at a dress shop. They were also union people—Helen's father worked at the post office. The rail people and the post office people had the best jobs in the black community.

We'd talk about everything that came along, families, kids, the price of things, everything families talk about. We didn't talk politics a lot because I was the only politician among us.

There was a bar on Lyndale and Olson Highway that opened up right after the lifting of Prohibition. I think it was called the Key Club. It was nice enough, ordinary place. Beers were ten, fifteen cents. At that time most everybody was drinking Grain Belt. I didn't particularly like it, but I drank it anyhow. Grain Belt was one of the first ones to come out with a strong beer after the depression. I got to a place where I liked Miller and Hamm's, the old established ones. I probably started doing Grain Belt because the plant was just around the corner in northeast Minneapolis.

My mother, before she died, she said, "Well, are you thinking of a family?" From the time I was nine, I'd tell her I'd like to have six kids and not get married. And she said, "Why?" I said I didn't want to bother with a man.

She said, "Well, if I were you, I'd think about that, considering the economic conditions." She said I should put the financial stuff together and maybe I'd want to rethink that. So I did. I just cut back in my mind from six to two.

But I never did have any children. The doctor said there was nothing wrong with my health except I couldn't have kids. Actually, what he said was, "There's not anything radically wrong with you, you just might not be able to get pregnant."

A lot of women in those days were told they had a "tilted womb," so they couldn't conceive. I remember he said something about a womb, but he didn't say what.

He said he would have to look around inside of me to find something exactly wrong with me, but I just ran out of money. I went to other doctors, but they also couldn't tell me what was wrong just by looking at me in their office. Of course, we didn't have the high-tech machines then that we do today, those computing machines that tell you about how to have babies.

This was quite a bit before the union had a health plan—I wasn't even in the union then. This was probably about 1932, 1933. I think if there would have been health insurance, if I would have had the money, I would have done something more. Considering how my health has turned out, it would've been nice to have kids—I would have liked to have passed on some of these genes!

Part of the reason I didn't do anything was the way my mother died so young the year before this, at forty-seven, in 1931, the year I was married. Death seemed to happen a lot then. My youngest sister, Dorothy, the one with eczema, died right after she was born, and Mom died about a year and a half later. I always wondered who had a hand in whose death, between Mom and Dorothy. Mom just couldn't get up in the morning. When she was dying, I went back home and stayed with her and my father for six months.

It turned out Mother had cancer in the reproductive organs. I didn't know about cancer or what it meant then. We didn't know what to do. There was no chemotherapy in those days. Both grandmas outlived her. Now you can see why I'm very concerned about health-care reform.

I did feel a stigma about not having kids, within my own family a little bit. It was not too bad. I'm one of these strong characters that lets that go in one ear and out the other. I liked kids, and always took care of the neighbors' kids, my sister's kids. I think I went through some pain—looking at other people in families, having kids, active in churches. I would've liked to have done the same thing.

I think I would have found ways to take care of the kids and found ways to be an activist. I know I wouldn't have been able to do the same activist things, but I would have tried.

My marriage to Clyde, it was about eight years. You know when you get away from that relationship, unless it was a wild bubbling affair, you don't remember dates too well.

Clyde and I had our problems. It was not bad to the point of violence, it was more of a real-world battle. I was just gone so much. It just kind of happened. I was moving up in the union, in politics, all of the time. It was different in his family. My family was always involved in education and politics, but even though Clyde's mother was a schoolteacher, she was never involved in politics. We started arguing in 1934, after I got involved in organizing the Athletic Club, and it sort of went downhill from there.

I never heard him say a woman's place was in the home, but I would suspect that. We'd never argue except when I was gone a lot, and I was gone every other night. I was working with the NAACP, as well as being on the board of the union, and the committees, too.

I just tried to explain the importance of being involved with labor, and he kept talking about cooking. I was pretty much of an old-fashioned kind of gal, about cooking, cleaning, and washing. I was cooking all the time. I may have resented whatever it was he said to me, that's what you do when you're married. It was something special, maybe, he wanted and I flew off the handle.

Clyde always said that he did want kids, but he had sort of a nervous breakdown late in the depression, and that was another stymieing factor as far as even adopting. There was a court case in 1939 or so, shortly before our marriage ended, where they accused him of chasing young kids in the park. I never really wanted to get mixed up in it, because I was working every day, but the case was never proved.

What happened was that he wasn't working. I don't know how he lost that car-polishing job. It seems to me he and the boys went out and got drunk. I would not call drinking a problem for him, but it happened periodically. My tolerance for alcohol was so low; it didn't take much to stop me. Anyway, he was sitting in the park every day. Any man that's got time on his hands could be a possibility for depression.

By that time, we were well along the process of not agreeing. I wasn't home like the traditional wife at a certain time, and I'd no more than get home from work, prepare some dinner quickly, then take off for a meeting. He didn't like that at all, but I wasn't going to change, and after eight years we agreed to part. That was 1939.

In 1941, my dad died of a heart attack—no one had any advance knowledge of that. We had these sixty-something men in good health, and then all of a sudden they were gone. I just felt it couldn't happen. My father was one of those people, he was so strong and so determined in everything he did, I took it for granted he was going to be there forever. I had visions of him being around his children and his grandchildren for a long, long time. When I saw him with the small number of grandchildren he had at that time, he really legitimized my vision.

It was hard for me when he died, really hard for me. He was a very strong person. I knew he was right all the time, so him passing was bound to shake a person. We talked things over all the time. I never had anyone like that ever again.

I was lonely without him. Remember, I used to drive home every other week. That was always good, whether it was family stuff or politics or whatever, it was always good for me to go there. It was great, just kind of lighthearted in a certain way. For example, I always liked Chevs, and the men in the family were Ford people, so we always got into that kind of silly argument.

The thing is, my dad had married again, and she didn't know a damn thing about farm life. The only reason we had some concern for her was that she was a good friend of my mother's sister, Aunt Eva. This woman was a lot younger. After he died, we had trouble with Isabelle—that was her name—because she was sashaying around the county making friends with people that we didn't give the time of day to. When she began making friends with a lawyer in Hinckley, we got suspicious. He was out to make money from breaking the farm up, we thought. She knew she had some of the farm's worth coming to her because of the marriage.

There were certain people living there who did want to see it divided. We had a good farm, one of the best farms in the county. If the farm split up, a lot of white people were interested in getting at it, out of racism for some, I'm sure. Gladys was easier to push around, to the way some community folks might have wanted, but Cortland was not budged from his positions. We kept that farm together.

We called in Dad's oldest brother, Uncle Walter, who was still living, and he had a lot of influence over Isabelle. I got everyone to the bank, we gave her one-third of what the farm was worth. We borrowed on it to give her cash. It came up to something like $23,000. It didn't affect farm operations at all because we didn't let it. We had good credit at banks in Sandstone, Pine City, and Hinckley, and could put together loans.

We then turned everything over to my oldest brother, Richard. I didn't want to be bothered by it—as a woman, I was not on secure ground to take it over, but for years the land was in my name. We gave it to Richard because we didn't want to run into any problems with would-be buyers. They might have gotten ideas to try to take it over if they saw it was headed up by a woman, even if that woman was me.

We'd gotten another eighty acres that Richard and Herbert bought. They were bound and determined that if anything happened to them, it should fit into the family, but if they died and there was ever any division, then Cortland would get the eighty acres. We kept the farm together after Richard died in the tractor accident. We just did it under the combined force of the four of us—we rented it out. Both the farms we had were together, the one-hundred-and-sixty-acre and the eighty-acre, they are still in the family.

We've rented to the same family for years, the Kapoff family. They raise mostly dairy, and they always pay the rent on time. They were believers in the dairy, because the Kapoff mother was an Irons, our neighbor in Pine County, and there was no straying from the dairy persuasion at all.

We would classify how our family worked today as community. Everybody knew their niche and they did it; it wasn't easy, but we did what we were supposed to do. There was no rebellion, but at the tail end of the thirties, Herbert and Richard went out and bought their own land, but they also helped the old man out from time to time when they left.

Dad did hire other help, but I think he felt a little disappointed that they left. Look, they just wanted that independence. On some other farms around there, the sons did the same thing, but they looked after their parents. They never talked to me about running their own show. They just went out and got their own farm.

Lee Johnson and I married in 1947. I was in my forties. I didn't think I'd get married again. I dated one of my brothers-in-law for one night before my sister met him. We went to the symphony and he bought me a box of candy, and that was it. It didn't go any further. I wanted to work politically, which wasn't him—though I loved the symphony.

I met Lee at some political thing, something that emanated from the U. He was a nice-looking, strong man. When he told me he was a cement finisher, I liked him better because I had designs on him for the union and politics. Why did I marry him? It was a combination of things. Every large contractor in Minneapolis liked Johnson. Whenever there were layoffs in the building trades—Cedarstrom, Knutson—they always had room for a good cement finisher.

I didn't date him that long because I was getting ready to put him in the union—the construction trades. That's true! He didn't have to marry me, but it made it better because I brought him right into the Central Labor Union. That's the coalition of locals within a jurisdiction; in Minneapolis it's the Central Labor Body, in St. Paul the Trades and Labor Assembly. I told my friends, here was a good man for the board of the Construction Trades, or something to the effect that he would be good for office. I remember one of the guys looking at me with a quizzical look, but as long as I was around, Lee was officer material! I was a political organizer even as I was getting married! I remember taking him to the Central Labor body meeting, and he said, "Gosh, what a setting—there's so damn much power in this room, they could do anything!"

Now with Lee, I was the person in charge. I was married to him for five years. It was the same thing—we just began to argue about being gone. He had been married before, with one child, a girl. I didn't want her staying at the house because she would upset everything and I knew how much time I'd spend taking care of a twelve-year-old—very rambunctious. I knew if I said yes to something, she would go to her dad and he would say no. I was too old to go through that.

After we divorced, I kind of stayed in touch with his sister. He went into the ministry after he left me. Boy, I took a ribbing for that from my friends—union people, community people in Minneapolis. They'd tell me, "You drove him all the way to the ministry."

I never met anyone else, at least anyone else who was not attached. Every once in a while I would see some good men around, and I would think, Why didn't I meet that person when I was younger?

Chapter 10

Meeting Hubert Humphrey

Swan Assarson, the man from Sweden who had given me the economic education, was eventually hired by our union, Local 665. We hired him as a business agent, and he was a key man in how I came to meet Hubert Humphrey.

I met Hubert about 1938. He was working at the U of M, where he was finishing up graduate work, on a Works Progress Administration project—his income to go to Macalester. At the U, he did a lot of teaching about how to create economic power for all.

Swan liked Hubert and had met him through some seminar at the U. Swan was plugging away for Hubert before I ever met him. It happened on campus. I had been to a meeting, the Young Democrats or the Young Communists—I liked to listen in on what all of them were saying. We were meeting on a lot that had no buildings on it, near one of the technical buildings. It was a gathering place for various people to stop and talk, run into people you knew. There were a lot of people there that called themselves leaders and authorities, but of course, a lot of people stood there and yelled to high heaven. Hubert sometimes would be one of them, I found out later. It was like a speaker's corner.

I was on my way to somewhere else, and many times I had stopped by. I ran into Swan, and *boom,* he introduced me to Hubert. I would suspect that Hubert knew Swan the way I knew him. Swan was very geared into young people, which Hubert was.

Swan said that Hubert was quite a person, a good politician, and quite a gentlemen. I thought he was too because he started talking and saying some darn good things. He was always talking about people—the equality of people, and good things for labor, and how wrong government was in that it wasn't able to provide an equal education. Well, this got me going right away.

My feeling was that Hubert was interested in running for office, and Swan was moving him toward that. I don't honestly know how he got all of this so well, coming from a little town in South Dakota. Knowing him a while, I know he was very curious about people and history. I guess he just learned about people well.

I've often thought about why Hubert was not in the Farmer-Labor Association, but the Democrats. Part of it, I guess, was because in the little town where he grew up, his father was a Democrat. It was kind of funny on the part of Hubert: he would say in these wide-open spaces—meaning South Dakota—he couldn't find another Democrat.

There were two basic things that Hubert and I fought for and were hard-nosed about that changed this country: the right of labor to organize, and the right of black people to live and not be hung from the hanging tree. Lynching was still big in the South. My family—I had my dad's relatives in Missouri and my mom's in Kentucky—they were out of the way of the Klan, but they were still in trouble. I was anxious to find all the allies among Democrats that I could get, because the Democratic Party had a lot of Southerners in it, and I always wanted more Democrats on the other side.

What I didn't realize is that Hubert was hanging on to me as much as I was hanging on to him. By then, I had been elected to the Local 665 board, one of five delegates from our local to the Central Labor Body. That was where the union power was—for me to get waiters and busboys jobs. But for him, he looked at my delegate spot and saw a way to get to a hundred and eighty thousand affiliated people in the Twin Cities and Minnesota. He saw the size of that membership. Naturally, that would excite him.

I was a natural for Hubert and I eventually heard by way of gossip that he was angling for higher office. We met in 1938, and by 1942 he had announced his candidacy for mayor of Minneapolis in 1943.

I just hit it off with him because of his philosophy. When he talked about equality, he was right on target. Outside of Floyd B. Olson, I hadn't heard any white candidate talk that way. That was how rare it really was then. He also said the right things about organized labor. He asked, how could you have equality without the lower fifty percent of society having good jobs? I really liked that he made the connection between lifting people up and jobs right away. He also never told the funny jokes most men told about women—that was one of the ways I knew he believed in equality. The fact that Hubert could tie it in with all the labor issues showed his basic humanitarian understanding.

When Hubert and I began plotting our course, we'd meet at a combination of places. There was a smaller building next to where the Orpheum Theater is. We had the whole third floor, with enough room for a davenport, but we never had enough floor space for a general assembly, full meetings. Hubert was in and out of there like it was a living room. There was also a pointed, triangular building at Seventh and First. Local 665 rented that as an assembly hall from the Teamsters, who also had meetings there. Anytime Hubert got the call that there was a meeting, he would drop in. There was always a big pot of coffee—our secretary kept a pot going all the time—and Hubert would just gab and hold court as long as that coffee held out. I used to call him the last of the great spellbinders. The union people got to know him real well.

We wouldn't necessarily agree on everything, especially the Young Communist League. I was really out of the Young Communist League when Hubert and I started getting together in 1938. Swan and I discussed the educational activities of the Young Communist League a lot over the years. What they were doing was mostly an educational body, on labor education as well as general education. They were very strong in the area of separation of church and state, and to keep religion and private schools from encroaching on the public schools.

What Hubert thought of the Young Communist League is kind of fuzzy in my mind. On some level, he was a Democrat, not a more left-wing person like a Farmer-Laborite. I think he worried about the

Communists being atheist and totalitarian, genuinely. I didn't see any of that totalitarianism in what they were trying to do here—and I said so, to more people than just Hubert. They talked about equality of education when most people wouldn't.

At our roots I was really very clean and pure, and so was Hubert. If there were any skeletons in the closet, people would have zeroed in on us, especially in the early years. But we saw ourselves in different ways: he was this academic from Mac, this intellectual from the U of M, and I was this radical farmer. Maybe we also saw our futures differently. I was an activist; you read those clichés that get attached to other people—the reds—and you knew you fit into that, too, but you didn't care because you believed in the good things you were working for. But Hubert had his eye on being an elected official, needing a majority of the public, and he wanted to make sure no one ever hung that red cliché on him because it could have sunk him.

Some of the arguments we'd have about Communists: I had to tell him, some of those people he was talking about was me! I was not at all ashamed to be called red. I never visualized attacks on so-called reds to the extent that other people did. Hubert, he was such a mixture, hot about communism but fighting so hard on jobs and education, which was a big issue for the so-called reds, too. Basically, ninety-nine percent of us were workers, and if we made it better for workers and the farm coalition, we'd make it better for everyone. I was coming out of the Farmer-Labor Association and the Non-Partisan League, and we believed in a lot of collectivism, and maybe Hubert felt that went too far.

Sometimes, it was also the rub between the working person and the thinking person—maybe the way I'd disagree with you if I was writing a contract. I'll give you an example of what I mean: we were at a social event and Doug Hall, who was our great labor lawyer, was telling us what we should have in our contract. Well, this was in the early days of our union, and that made us feel so indignant! A bunch of us said, "Let us write our own contract, and you keep us legal!" We did not want to have someone on retainer take us over to tell us what was right. I think there were times when Hubert and I disagreed on strategy or something, and I just felt my head was more in the noose.

After an argument, we'd realize we didn't really differ on the important philosophical things, like equal opportunity, just about how to get there. Hubert always came back to this when we were done talking. He'd always end up saying, "Well, it's the right thing to do."

Right from the first day Hubert was born he was some kind of a human being, but certain legislation on education, employment, health care, he got very sophisticated on that. Hubert would show great maturity in how to understand it from a negotiator's point of view, and then how to sell it to everyone. He sponsored laws to help us where we were going with our contracts—health benefits, working conditions. Why should you have to negotiate it when you can legislate it and make it law?

— Chapter 11 —

Union Equality

After we won at the Athletic Club and organized Local 665, I was working very hard at spreading unions around the town. I was pretty sure of myself. The whole spying thing that Robert Carothers wrote about actually came later on, after I was in the Young Communists, when I was on the board of Local 665.

One of the business agents for the union came out of northern Minnesota, and he was involved in gossip about spies. He said they've got a guy on who was a spy. They meant that the FBI had a person on the board—I still don't know who it was. My comment was, so what? What would we do differently? We'll still work for the betterment of working-class people.

Three or four of us officers would go out and have coffee together, you made sure you stuck together so nothing tricky could happen. I'm pretty sure one of them wasn't the infiltrator. You know your people, if you've been there since the inception. You pretty much know your people, because they've been tested and tried.

The thought crossed my mind that I could be arrested, but it didn't bother me and it still doesn't. My analysis is that it's good enough to say what is right or wrong. As I said, I got that from my dad. And how could I think about getting arrested, a young person like I was? It never bothered me—but I probably didn't have enough sense about it.

I was more worried about my safety for other reasons. Cecil Newman and I, we would write these pro-labor editorials. Cecil was a grassroots person. But when we would distribute our literature, I didn't like the idea of being out after dark. The Mafia was very strong then in Minneapolis, not the Italian Mafia, the Jewish Mafia. After nine o'clock, when it got dark in the summer, I just didn't go out.

I heard about both the Jewish and Italian Mafia attempting to get into unions, about the meetings in the pool halls of the Jewish Mafia, because I was right there. People would say that's where the radical Mafia meets, right there on Olson Highway, in the billiard room by my apartment! These meetings also used to be in an old theater, the Liberty Theater, or in some commercial buildings, if they were vacant. Anyplace where people congregated—and that was Jewish-owned.

I got rumors of mob influence on unions in Minneapolis—most of the information came from New York and places like that. It did happen here, just by mob types being too close to labor, preaching virtues of labor, food, and housing without really meaning it, things like that. I would not have listened if I had heard from the mob one-on-one, or if someone had stood on my feet, or tried to shake my shoulders. Nobody tried to influence me.

I became vice president of Local 665 ("that was as high as a woman could get then"; MWP). It took me eighteen months or two years to get there in the late thirties. We had another woman committed to equal pay that worked out of 458, the Cooks and Waiters. Her name was Ann Manley and she worked at the 620 Club. We communicated constantly. Basically, we wanted to make it pay off with equal wages for women. Ann was an ordinary hardworking gal; she did not have too much vision, but she was nice and believed in treating people right. She learned ten times from me what I learned from her, but she was a good talker, a vice president of 458. People that talk halfway decent can get put on anything.

I was on the entertainment committee. Now, you might not think that sounds powerful. I didn't know anything about entertainment, but I said, what do I do? They put on the Christmas party for union members. Right away, my ears went straight up. I thought that was a powerful position for getting union members' whole families involved, feeling connected.

I didn't care what the office was! What I'm known for in Minnesota is that all you have to do is make Nellie Stone Johnson thirty-second vice president and I'll gather all the power I need!

I was getting to know the families, and I was organizing the family. I used that as an organizing tool to appeal to members. That was a big part of the union itself, and we all had certain agendas to work from. Our dues at that time to our local weren't very much, around three dollars a month. The traditional thing was you'd get a couple of business officers working for unions—we hadn't yet negotiated a labor contract. That money was really for a Christmas party for kids. Every year, we had the Christmas party, and I would start working on members' families on the first of December. We had to make the decorations, decide what gifts to pass out, which hall to use, and so forth.

Most us women leaders kind of slipped in the back door. The back door was the lesser offices. Most of us were vice presidents or secretaries, members at large, trustees. See, there were not too many animals like myself. I knew that being a voting member of the executive board, I could do what I wanted.

Often it seemed like I was it, the only woman. One reason I never stopped, as I moved to state level, the national level, was that I wanted to find out where we were going and what we should be wanting to do.

Part of what helped was my continuing education. A lot of campuses were just frothing at the mouth to put their labor centers together in the thirties. Every Ivy League school tried to outdo the others with a labor conference during the thirties, during the Roosevelt administration.

I was on the Columbia University campus in New York. They had some damn good professors who were analyzing where we should go. They provided good economics professors for the most part. They just took you by the hand and taught you about the economic ABCs. Then some taught about the importance of organization. That was good.

Very few people know the fundamentals of what labor and politics are all about—caucuses, labor, organization of politics. I wouldn't get paid for this; I paid myself on this. I say that because most of that I did at my own expense.

I couldn't go to Harvard, or Princeton, Cornell, because I couldn't raise the money. My unions would help, but they couldn't pay for it all. I made it to the University of Chicago and Northwestern, too. We had things at the U, some through the Young Communist League.

My goal was to become very powerful in labor and politics. I was thinking about what it would be like if I ran for office. I thought I needed to know everything about politics—the history of blacks and Native Americans. It's important because you want everyone out there voting, and I had two or three strains of Native American blood. My main underlying goal was equality—I felt it very strong. My mother was a college grad in 1902, and my two grandmas dabbled around in teaching, and I thought I did need a better education. I wanted to be out there on the cutting edge of thinking, so when I said something to people, I wanted to have all the authority in the world.

People saw me involved, and eventually some said why not join the Farmer-Labor Association? Basically, that was the political education arm of the union movement, which was within the F-L Party. One of the advantages I had over most of our membership was that I was a minority person. I had to understand what it took to stay afloat in this society, politically. Unfortunately, most of the white women didn't have a clue of what they could use to get power and opportunity. For me, organization was always the key.

As an officer, I was part of the Central Labor Body, which was the group of all unions in Minneapolis. In 1938, I put them on record as being in support of hiring minority women as teachers. There were none that I knew of in Minneapolis. It seems to me that as soon as we passed our union resolution, Minneapolis did the hiring. Those things were hard because you always would risk bringing ninety percent of the delegation down on your head—the men part—and you didn't know if you'd get tripped going down the stairs. The mind-set for discrimination was there, but a lot of people wanted to be exposed to equal opportunity, too.

When I finally brought it up in the Central Body, it passed. I did something there unorthodox on that resolution to support equal opportunity. I didn't put that in resolution form in front of my own union, which you were supposed to do first. I just took it to the Central Body floor. But when I did bring it up there, then six or seven other people from my union, well, they hit the ground running to build up support. I was not a gutless person at all when it comes to dealing with humanity.

Back then, there were two constituencies that were not hired, Jewish and black women. They were not hired though they were well qualified. But out of that motion came many changes. That was mostly because, in city elections, labor had tremendous power, maybe a hundred thousand voters, and the policy makers knew it.

When it passed in the Central Body, it meant every local could support candidates who supported this sort of equal opportunity. There was always a debate on things like this. The thing was, we had tough people in our union. We were up against all these people—the conservative, racist union people—who didn't want to go through fighting with us again.

One of the things that helped us was that for years and years, I was vice chair of the local joint union board, then moved to the union organization statewide, their executive board, and I was president of that for a while. Once you get into those things, you know what battles you can fight.

We as people fought those battles for equal treatment every day. By the time we took action on a policy position, all you had to do is throw a policy into line, and the resolution would go through.

I'm sure my father ran up against the same argument about the price of wheat. You'd see him on the floor and he'd say, "You want to eat, don't you? Well, work for an organization to feed people."

One of the things I'm proudest of was that I was one of the first women on a contract negotiating committee. My groundwork was to talk about how all our top executive committee members were all members of our negotiating committee. So, I got to be vice president of the union, and it was automatic that I was a negotiator. It's hard to become a part of the policy making, but once I was part of that, it was not hard to become part of a negotiating committee.

We union members made the executive board contract negotiators bargain for equal pay for women in 1940—one of the first unions to do that. No matter what kind of fight I got into with the feminists down the road, they always liked that. A lot of times we would argue about them wanting to pass over black males—they had a whole lot of questions and reasons for not fighting that fight.

I had seen a bit of passing over black males at the Minneapolis Athletic Club in the thirties. There were secretaries fighting to get more money, to raise their profession up, but they wouldn't support raising a porter up. They did it to save themselves, make sure they got their money. But the black men were paid so little because there was so little opportunity, not because of the work!

Janitors, porters, red caps on the trains—they were the most educated black men in the country, doing menial work because of racism. That discrimination got to be something of a joke. We'd say, since young black men so often got jobs on the railroad, that we had the best educated railroad staff in the world!

Now, the women never put it to me that bluntly—that they didn't want black men raised up—but it was always, why should we include this category, that category in wage parity? They were the black male categories.

The whole class of women was quite a bit different then. It didn't matter how much academics you had. Most women were discriminated against in the general area of education—like the black men were with jobs, women were not offered an equal chance to go to college. I used that academic side of the debate to the hilt. Black men had it while most of the white women hadn't set foot in college, so why didn't black men get more?

What it showed was that we didn't quite have the support for the total equality of people; some of us were not willing to reach everyone up. Finally, those of us in the union who were for total equality were powerful enough in the leadership to demand that all groups were raised up, including janitors. This is what I mean about organizing—even in our union, you had to win positions of leadership to get everyone lifted up.

I was always trying to sell the idea of equality within a union or central body, and I always had to fight for the support of a section of women. I was one of the founders of the Minnesota Coalition of Trade Union Women, and I had a hard time getting the issue of equality for everyone across the board in 1972! They're still dragging their feet today!

The Minnesota Coalition of Trade Union Women is for women who were already organized into labor. They formulated their own coalition, not to set up their own policy, but to adhere to a labor policy, to direct votes—but not necessarily to make endorsements. They would not endorse unless they had people like me charging around. Our group was to organize women to be active within labor, and bound to the concepts and platform within labor.

There were some activities nationally. I wanted them to be a little bit more aggressive in formulating policy, on their caucuses, their committees, on their contract committees. It was a double whammy for me, because if the overall majority of women were lacking, then the women of color were definitely lacking, too.

I think women have more of a voice now, but aren't as strong as they could be. The only thing that will change it is more activities around the issues of women—more like in the American Federation of Teachers Local 59 out of Minneapolis. They negotiate contracts, and they have a few women who do it, but no women of color, I think. They at least don't have a Native American or a black there, so they are far from doing the job they should be doing on equal opportunity.

For a lot of people affirmative action is a misnomer. People say it's quota. In the Democratic Party, when I went to work there, women were demanding fifty percent representation as delegates and on committees, but they weren't demanding any percentages for women of color. I think that's one of the big weaknesses in the educational unions. Quotas for women, but not equal opportunity.

There's a reason I'm so hard on feminists—the racism there was so bad. It was almost the same as the good old boys before the laws on equal opportunity were on the books.

Negotiating meant you sat around those tables sometimes hours and hours. When you hear about the hours that Northwest Airlines union reps go through today, well, we went through everything just like that. A lot of times, our proposal on the right rate of pay really got chopped down.

We never did go out for drinks to hobnob with the bosses like some unions did. We had our own group that would go out and drink. We didn't hate each other to the point that we would kill each other, management and labor, but we didn't fraternize. Sometimes, the lawyers would get carried away, but there was generally not too much swearing.

They were pretty much people I'd put into one basket—the enemy basket. I'm sure they did the same thing to us. You could almost go by newspapers, remarks out of the corporate world. There was nobody I completely respected on that side, but two or three people came from the board of the Athletic Club that I thought were fairly decent people.

The thing was not just money, but a good health program. The question was how much would be paid by the employers. At that time, outside of the Teamsters, nobody really had this kind of health program. It began to grow, and before you knew it everyone was after a health program.

There's not an argument we didn't come up against, but we negotiated and negotiated and negotiated until we broke through. This was one of the lowest-paid industries, and we tried to take that into account just by arguing that they should be good human beings. There were some threats to strike, but we never did it.

All males on the board there got nice treatment, but all the women—

well, it didn't matter if they were white, you were kind of ignored in a nice way, a halfway nice way. They just didn't call you a bitch. Did Nellie Stone Johnson have trouble getting heard? No. I could yell like a bull moose, and all my barnyard stuff came back to me.

We had a man that came on the union executive board, he was a faculty member at Morris. After we became good beer-drinking friends, he said, "Oh they got their window dressing there," when he first saw me. "But after the first meeting, I heard you open your mouth and bellow out, and I realized you weren't what I thought you were." I didn't necessarily do the most talking, but when I talked, it usually set pretty good.

After we got our equal pay contract with the hotels, we did the negotiating with the insurance company. This was for the whole state of Minnesota, with all the various locals of the Hotels and Restaurant Workers Union. Statewide I became vice president and then president of the Minnesota Culinary Council.

The Teamsters had the best program in the late thirties, so what we did is, we looked to see what they were doing. The way it worked then was that a certain amount would go to us, on a checkoff system, that we would spend on health insurance. We would buy it ourselves. I didn't like the checkoff system, though, because it made our officers lazy people. A checkoff at the door, instead of organizing individually, is what happened. We got soft on meeting people individually, and that led to weaknesses down the road. Some of our leaders just counted the money and that was it.

The way we did the health deal is that the union met with somebody at the insurance company who was authorized to negotiate our contract. We went to Prudential and the old Metropolitan Life Insurance, and they turned us down. The companies said they just didn't write those policies; they did it for business, for the Chamber of Commerce, but not for the union.

Back in my farm days, the Metropolitan Life Insurance Company had a lot of blacks sewn up from the early days of insurance. It was just part of the black culture—if you had life insurance, you had it with them. The Metropolitan never recognized you as black, just a farmer. They gave policies that had no designs on nationality, one of the few. When one of my brothers died, we looked at his policy and there was no nationality on it.

But it was different, getting insurance for Nellie the union person as opposed to as a farmer. We ended up taking a big trip up to Winnipeg, Canada, to get a health insurance policy in our 665 contract—I think that was 1940 or 1941. I loved riding the trains!

The company was Great Western of Canada. At that time, the Canadian government was not that far away from being a socialist government. It was ironic when you considered that their country was governed by a king and queen! I suppose even the worst have streaks of goodness.

All the insurance companies finally had to come around. I think the ones who said no, they succumbed to racism and classism about the union and who was in it. The people we negotiated with didn't fall in for a lot of racism and classism. The three unions that we were negotiating for had seventeen thousand members! That was a lot of business for the enlightened few. Can you imagine someone turning down seventeen thousand customers today?

Chapter 12

DFL Merger

In 1943, the Farmer-Labor Party had lost two consecutive gubernatorial elections, after winning four in a row dating from Floyd B. Olson's 1930 breakthrough. An election is a lifetime in politics, and two is an eternity, even back in the days when governors were elected every two years. Faced with the prospect that they might be slipping into a permanent minority, Farmer-Laborites began to consider a merger with the weaker Democrats, who hadn't occupied the governor's chair since 1915. Another inspiration was Franklin Delano Roosevelt, who had held the presidency for three terms with a national Democratic coalition that included traditional party members as well as minor-party radicals.

The year 1858 is probably the last year I would have been comfortable as a Republican—but I wasn't a Democrat, either, until we merged the Farmer-Labor part with them to form the Democratic-Farmer-Labor Party in 1944.

The biggest thing you need to know about me partywise up to this point is that I was part of the Farmer-Labor Association. The Farmer-Labor Association was formed to teach the membership about the economic and social issues playing into the economic side—getting rid of racial and gender discrimination, and a thousand other things. Most member organizations paid dues to be part of the education association, not the party itself. Some farmers paid, but despite our name, it was mostly labor.

As I've told you, the people in the old Farmer-Labor Party were very basic, humane people. They wanted a job and a protection around that job and as much protection around public education. Those were not as big for the Democrats. The national Democrats were inclined to be much more conservative—especially on racial matters, coming out of the slavery that they ruled over in the South.

Some people in the labor movement started talking about a merger in 1943. Hubert Humphrey was talking to some people in the Democratic Party about it at the same time.

The biggest thing that got us together was Franklin Roosevelt's fourth try for the White House in 1944. You've got to remember, FDR's election wasn't a sure thing; he was getting old, and no one ever had a fourth term ever before.

> The opposition was coming on strong against Roosevelt when they started setting up these various groups for Roosevelt. A member of the . . . we now call them the radio-TV evangelists—Father Coughlin from Michigan and the House of the Little Flower or something like that. Every week he pounded against Roosevelt, even to the point of baiting him, like his name wasn't Roosevelt, it was Rosenthal or Rosenberg or something like that. They baited him and just pounded away at that awful stuff. (MHS, 36–37)

We expected a strong showing of some of the Republicans, especially the Chamber of Commerce and the National Association of Manufacturers. They were almost animalistic in pressing their initiatives; we felt like we were fodder, like under a German tank!

To a lot of Farmer-Laborers, FDR was the first Farmer-Labor president, though he certainly didn't call himself that. There was the big issue of keeping Social Security, which wasn't very old at that point, to help working people take care of themselves after retirement. Of course, FDR was solid on labor issues. He got laws passed to allow unions more power to bargain collectively, and to protect our members from being fired for organizing, as I had been the first time around at the Athletic Club. He hated big business, and we liked how he controlled them.

Here's another thing that was going on. World War Two was winding down, and there were some debates going on about world organizations, such as the Dumbarton Oaks conference, which became the United Nations. We were internationalist, and so were the FDR Democrats. You know all the labor unions have international in their name somewhere, even though they don't do a lot about that, this was one time to prove it. We wanted a World Bank to back up the money, so that working-class people's savings would be safe and there'd be some security, unlike that debacle in 1929.

We didn't want to lose what we gained as working-class and people of color. FDR had signed an executive order in 1941, Executive Order 8802—I'll never forget the number. It banned civil rights discrimination in federal defense contracts. [The Brotherhood of Sleeping Car Porters' A. Philip Randolph had threatened a march on Washington to embarrass the Roosevelt administration if they didn't do this. Randolph's plan became the inspiration for the massive March on Washington during the sixties civil rights struggle.]

Executive Order 8802 was what we modeled our own Minneapolis Fair Employment Practices Act on in 1947. Until we got civil and human rights things done in the public sector, we would never get things done in the private sector. And of course, FDR got the public employees the right to organize, which they didn't have until then.

What Franklin didn't have, we had Eleanor for. She was the one leading the charge for the equality of blacks and women, that they should get an equal shake in all employment.

I belonged to a second group, the National Black Caucus, the black caucus associated with the NAACP, sort of the political arm. I was voted on from the Minneapolis branch. I remember Bill Dawson out of Chicago—he later became Congressman Dawson—when he was the National Black Caucus president. He was playing around with the officialdom of the Democratic Party. We were all working for the Black Caucus to help elect Roosevelt in late 1943 and 1944. I became his secretary. I never wanted to be a secretary, and I was probably the worst secretary they ever had! I remember telling people during meetings to slow down what they were saying. I wanted to get involved with policy, the mouthy part, if you know what I mean.

The big thing we did was to be sure that eligible black voters were registered, and that they voted for FDR. We just went crazy wild in every state that had any contingency of black activist people. We all worked our own communities; that's what we had as a directive. We got the word out through organizations, churches, the NAACP, the Urban League, and a lot of labor people. The labor people were the key people in the NAACP.

There were hard-nosed labor people who did not want to join the Democrats, who were not too well thought of in those days. They did not like the Bilbos and the Rankins of the Southern congressional delegations. There was so much racism in all the Southern states, just a complete denial of hiring people of color, having a job. That's about the most devastating thing you can do—the most violent thing you can do to people is not let them have a job. The antimerger argument was that the stuff we were arguing for, equality and the right to unionize, was not supported in the South, and a lot of Democrats here in Minnesota were also very quiet about those issues. We built some pretty strong people in the F-L Party, and from a humanitarian position, we damn well knew we were right.

The Democrats here, well, they were often the same type of business people as the Republicans, only with a little more humanity, which is why the Farmer-Labor Party stuck around so long.

But I felt that we had to come together as working-class people in coalitions, for Franklin Roosevelt, and for people like Hubert Humphrey, because even though we didn't know he was running for the Senate, we knew he'd be running for something big. It was just raw pragmatism to me.

Now even though everyone today kind of drops off the Farmer-Labor part of the DFL, in the early 1940s, the Farmer-Labor Party was much stronger than the Democrats. When the question of the merger came up, there wasn't much to the Democrats at that time in

Minnesota. Maybe one reason I didn't care so much which side won going in, was that it wasn't hard to understand who would be the leader in this outfit. We Farmer-Laborers were the ones with the direct contact with labor, and there was a big labor membership in Minnesota. We were contributing more—we had the population and the education side of it. We in labor carried a double role—family-type farmers and labor. It was very hard to find people from outside the metro area who weren't a combination of family-type farmers and labor. I didn't really buy the argument about what we'd lose because we'd put up good candidates that we elected, like Floyd B. Olson and Hjalmar Petersen. That's why the Democrats wanted in; a lot of times politics is just a simple matter of counting.

I told people in the Farmer-Labor Party that we wouldn't lose anything here in Minnesota, and we'd maybe influence the national scheme. And Hubert proved that in 1948 with his civil rights speech that moved the Democratic Party forward.

As an officer of my union, I was a delegate to the Farmer-Labor Association, and so I was in a position to be one of the people chosen by my local membership to be on the merger committee. Every local that was a member of the Farmer-Labor Association had the privilege of selecting merger committee members. I was kind of a consensus choice. Our union also chose Ray Wright, who was the business agent of 665, and Doug Hall, who was our union counsel.

We made the issues of what was closest to our hearts. What was closest to mine were jobs for women and people of color, the wage structure, health programs, vacation time, the same left-wing stuff we're wrestling with now. That's what I wanted in a merged DFL.

I've thought about it a lot since the merger, that maybe we in labor had more power then because we had a damn good platform—since the election of Floyd B. Olson. FDR had had his eye on Floyd B. Olson for the next president. He could see that progress for labor would be carried on, and that wielded a lot of power with us in the F-L. Of course, Floyd B. got cancer and died in 1936. But those were the sorts of ties between FDR's version of the Democrats and Floyd B's F-Lers. That carried a lot of power between the parties, a large amount of philosophical power.

The leadership of both parties were worried who the merger would favor. Everybody always asks me who won in the merger, and it didn't matter to me as long as we in the Farmer-Labor Party got a lot of its platform in.

It seemed to me that we met forever during the merger talks. We met every Sunday morning at the Y on Ninth in downtown Minneapolis. It was against the rules, because you're not supposed to do political meetings there. I got tired of getting up early every Sunday morning, because I needed the rest after a long work week! You could tell working-class people were involved because we had to meet on Sundays; today, a bunch of lawyers and hirelings could meet whenever they wanted to! We met there, because for those of us who got up early without eating breakfast, there was a cafeteria. You could get breakfast, take it to your table, and eat while everyone talked.

On most Sunday meetings, we had twenty people—sometimes less, sometimes more. Ray Wright and I were always there. Sometimes Hubert came in. He would come in and talk, naturally. He would try to reason with us. He was just for a merger. He picked out a sore spot for many of us and said, "I don't like the Southern Democrats either," but he felt Roosevelt was a necessity. Of course, he had run for mayor and lost a year earlier, so he wanted a united party for the 1945 city elections.

Being with the Southern Democrats was definitely a two-way street. Me and my father's generation, we had given up a lot—time and work—to build a Farmer-Labor Party that had no racist mentality in it. But my role on the merger committee was to support the basic philosophy, the right of working-class men and women to organize across the board. I wanted equality for women, which we were not getting from the Democrats at the time, and equality of people of color.

That's why Hubert Humphrey made a great spectacle on equality—

to bring the groups together. Hubert Humphrey spouted all of the stuff, but he also believed it. I was a dirt farmer—that's what the family farmers referred to ourselves as—and there was a great love for Humphrey among farmers, too. I don't think there was a closer friendship than him and William Thatcher, president of the Farmers Union for what seemed like a hundred years.

We had very strong labor people fighting against the merger— Robley Cramer, publisher of the *Labor Review* newspaper and an organizer for the Central Labor Body, plus Roy Wier, who became a member of Congress. He was a combination of guts and graciousness. He roared like a lion to people who tried to make it more academic than just feeding people. He and Red Cramer argued very hard on that point in the so-called merger committee. He said we had to keep a strong philosophy of labor if we merged—that was just fundamental.

I honestly do not remember dropping anything out of the Farmer-Labor's major things. The hard thing was the party echelon, who the national party people would be. We had our Socialist Norman Thomas people in the Farmer-Labor Party, somewhat like the Progressive Party people in Wisconsin, and then our own Farmer-Labor philosophy. Most of the compromising was done on party positions, not on principles. The Democrats were mostly about getting patronage jobs; they were the insiders, the muckety-mucks that got work when there was a Democrat in the White House.

To show you how strong we were, out of those haggling sessions at the Y, the first chairman of the merged party was George Phillips, the head of the Central Labor Body, an electrician who worked for NSP, and who of course was a Farmer-Labor member. The fact that he was labor sold him to most of us. I think he was a little less radical because he worked for NSP—that shaded it a bit with a certain amount of conservatism. I think that a lot of times, but not every time, you can tell where people are coming from by where they work. The utility was pretty conservative, and so were many of their unions. That made George safe to a lot of the Democrats, too. He was seen as being less hateful to business than some of us.

We spent a whole lot of other time on the other positions—the person who came out of milk drivers of St. Paul, who was the first vice president, second vice president, things like that. We knew what we wanted, and the only way to get that in a merger was hard numbers that counted.

We brought the two groups together in 1944; the Democrats were meeting at the old Radisson Hotel in downtown Minneapolis, while the Farmer-Laborers were at the old Nicollet Hotel. I remember Elmer Benson, who was the last F-L governor, leading the charge. He said we're adjourned, or dismissed, and we marched up to meet the Democrats at the Radisson. We met to finish off the convention at the Radisson, and it was very exciting for me. It was also very tiring, because we got out of there at two A.M.! We had to argue more about turf, about how to structure delegations, the officialdom of the party, anything that was not all worked out in advance.

Chapter 13

First Elected Black in Minneapolis

One June 12, 1945, just weeks after World War II ended in Europe and Franklin Roosevelt's death, Minneapolis newspaper headlines heralded the election of thirty-four-year-old DFLer Hubert Humphrey as mayor of Minneapolis; Humphrey demolished the incumbent Republican 61 to 39 percent. But the secondary headline featured "City Elects First Negro in Library Board Contest." Nellie not only won, she topped the field, including the most popular library board incumbent. The Morning Tribune *described her philosophy this way: "To her, books and education are the greatest forces in bringing about an understanding of all human relationships and in providing equality of opportunity." The story limited Nellie to one quote about her new duties overseeing the Minneapolis public library system: "She echoes the late Franklin Roosevelt's definition: 'Books are weapons in a democracy.'"*

One day in 1945, this wild man, the Swedish business agent Swan Assarson, said to me, "Nellie, you should run for office." This was something that told you how progressive Swan was, because if I won, I would be the first black elected to a Minneapolis city office.

Swan was pretty old by that time—I think he died when he was seventy or seventy-two, maybe, in the early 1950s. We tried to hang out a lot. We'd meet over coffee, to discuss history, and I guess just continue our continuing education. We talked a lot of world history. He seemed to know how every country in the world functioned as far as labor and the power structure. We never really joked around. I wanted to know, and he really wanted to tell.

One of the things he enlightened me about was Sweden. I had always read about what a democratic history Sweden had, that the lesson of Swedes was how they treat each other, regardless of class. But he would tell me about a time when Swedes enslaved Swedes, very similar to what happened to blacks in the South, when people were not born with their own names. That amazed me.

Local 665's headquarters was at Ninth and Hennepin, on the third floor of that corner building next to the Orpheum. We had kind of an old-fashioned parlor room in one of those rooms, with a davenport, and a lot of scattered straight chairs.

It was probably there that he told me what he wanted me to do, and I said I wanted to run for Minneapolis school board. But I had helped to put together a coalition slate among labor for the school board, and there was no point in me muddying up the waters. The Central Labor Body had picked a slate already, and they wanted three people from different walks of life to support—the wife of a construction worker, another union person, and a younger businessperson. The businesspeople brought a lot of votes to the whole slate, and education was a place where labor broadened its base.

So I said I would just go for the library board. I didn't want to be foolhardy and split the labor vote. I figured that the library board was not too far removed from the school board. Whatever you do from there, you can do from the library position.

And there was a chance to do some serious education and training. The library board was not only elected people, but the superintendent of the Minneapolis school district, and the president of the U of M board of regents. I figured I could do my education thing about equal opportunity, because to some of those high people, we were still living in the days of slavery or anti-Semitic times. A lot of people said the U was anti-Semitic, that they had a quota system, a low quota, for Jews in medicine and the law. Of course, black people didn't even figure into a quota.

All through my life, I believed that if I just rubbed elbows with the powerful, something good would come of it. That doesn't mean I didn't try to work them hard, but there was something to be gained just by getting them to associate with different kinds of people.

I do think rubbing elbows with the likes of me pushed Hubert Humphrey toward the great 1948 speech he made about civil rights at the Democratic convention. How in the world would people like Hubert Humphrey really know about me otherwise? You may understand the rights of all people, but you can't really feel how important those rights are unless you get to know different kinds of people. Hubert Humphrey listened when I talked about it. They talked about how much he talked, but they don't realize how much he listened.

Hubert also was one of the first ones who wanted me to run, partly because I would be the first black elected to office in Minneapolis, and because I could speak for labor and equality from experience. I told Hubert, "It sounds good, but tell me what I need." Believe it or not, I didn't know a lot about organizing a political race at this time. I knew about union work, about getting out the vote, but not running a whole race.

Hubert said, "No skeletons, be willing to run, and, I guess, read and write." Now, he didn't insult me by saying that last part—he was just making a point about how basic the qualifications really were. Years later, we were at the union office on Lyndale and Hennepin Avenue. We were supporting a member of the Teamsters, it could've been for the library board. Well, I remember someone from the teachers union said, we in education don't mind you being in labor, but can you read and write? Now that was a different thing. There was an undercurrent of elitism from the white-collar unions toward the blue as far as I was concerned. There was always an undercurrent of classism in people, even labor people, of course.

Labor had screened me—that means they interview you before endorsing you, to see if you uphold labor's positions—and they wanted to ask about the skeletons, too. Mob corruption, stealing some money, killing or beating up people, things like that. They wanted to make sure something like that would have no negative impact on labor, since I was going to be kind of a high-profile candidate by virtue of my race. I don't think anybody asked me about being with the Communist Party at that screening.

Looking back on it now that kind of checking seems funny, me being such a longtime labor person, but they were careful and didn't assume anything. For the first screening, I couldn't get off work, so Swan went for me. Later, I went for myself.

They couldn't find any skeletons—except, for some of them, one that was right out in the open: me being a woman. I was used to that to the hilt! Some labor folks, even if they accepted women in, didn't want them running anything. Again, it wasn't anything said exactly. I told the ones who turned up their noses, if being a woman is derogative, then I'm a big, bad woman!

But labor, they were beginning to feel signs of the times changing. And several of the screening people, they said, "Library board, that's a good spot for a woman." I understood what they were saying—it really wasn't that important a job, but it was male chauvinism. But you remember what I said about the thirty-second vice president in my union. I didn't mind taking lower-ranked jobs to get into the power structure. I got questions about being black, too, but it was kind of veiled and not necessarily negative.

Within labor, being a woman caused some trouble, but when I was running, some talk about me being black got very negative in the wider community. The person who was the head librarian at the time, a man named Carl Vitz, he saw cause to send a letter to the *Minneapolis Tribune*, raising questions about my ability to handle dollars. Because I wasn't white! That's about what it boiled down to. I thought, you son of a gun, you! It was a surprise, but my mother always said consider the source. She said sometimes the academics are the ones with no horse sense. He had to be pretty academic to get the job, but didn't show much common sense. Common sense has to go along, almost on an equal basis, with intellect.

Ray Wright, our local business agent, said maybe we could make a point back at him by raising some question of him, his academic abilities. Actually, we used the immigrant issue to turn that around. We said, well, he was an immigrant, and what are his chances to be smart academically because of his immigrant background? We didn't believe that, of course, but it made our point about ignorant prejudice.

Other than that letter, I never encountered open racism. There was a local radio host named Luke Radar [an evangelist for the River-Lake Gospel Tabernacle], he was kind of like that Father Coughlin.

> Luke Radar endorsed me and Hubert, so I said, we don't need him....
> It was a clever thing he did, because I think he thought that we would
> be two people that couldn't be beat, you know, and it would show
> some kind of progressive movement on his part. So he picks us out
> of the whole group of DFLers and endorsed us. I was scared to death
> of that endorsement! (MHS, 37)

A lot of people at the time thought I was just a peon, but they underestimated me. I never made any bones about my background as a farmer. I don't care if people are city folks, or the educated elite—they have some farming back in their history. We are all descendants of a farm economy, and folks were even closer to those roots when I was running. And there were still some farms in the city. Where Northtown Mall is, that remained farmland back then. I would talk about the right of the family farmer to get a fair price, which showed I understood how equality affected them, and that would get me my city votes fifty-five years ago.

These connections between issues, there was actually much more humaneness then than now. They weren't so dog-eat-dog or selfish like a lot of people today, who've made it because of what those good folks did then. Now you have to justify helping people a lot more.

For the election, we only had a few weeks to work—I suppose that was good for a first-time race. I was pragmatic putting together my first campaign. I did it by feel. I was working every day, then I would go to four or five meetings, and then be fresh for work the next day. It was really something! One of the things that kept me going, even though

I didn't need much help with that, was that Hubert Humphrey was at the top of the ticket, running for mayor after he had lost in 1943. Hubert and I campaigned for all three school board members—that was a big election too that year—and all the city folks on the DFL slate worked for me. I thought it was really great, I was glad to see the top man on the ticket out there for me.

If you got two people in town together, we were there, Hubert and I. It didn't require any bombasting by us, even though you might not believe that when Hubert was involved. Mostly, we just told people the platform and worked our working-class base.

I told people about the labor platform, and Hubert pretty much adopted the fundamentals of the New Deal. I told people when I ran that the library was an extension of the school board. It had to be open to all and well funded so that people of modest means would have this vast knowledge at their disposal. Schools were to tell people what to go after, but libraries were the place to get it. It was a clear extension of the classroom education. That was one of the reasons I agreed to switch to it in the first place.

I know I talk all the time about equal education for all, but saying that everyone should have education was a hard, real issue in those days. Fifty percent of the people had no access to higher education—people in the working class, financially. The denial that existed then about equal access was like the denial about the black community today, where schools aren't equal and financial hurdles are so high.

As far as women in those days, women were so low down it was pitiful. There were only certain jobs they could have, and certain types of education were withheld. The proof is the lack of women in math and science; that still happens today, and only after a generation of feminism are you starting to see it change. Hubert was all for women. I used to tell him that he was almost a suffragette!

I've got to admit, it was mostly academic people involved in my campaign, which kind of rankled me because we wanted more rank and file. The people at the U really zeroed in on my race. It gave them a chance to show the world how liberal they were—I knew that. They just had to be there. There was a man, Dr. Theodore Brammel, who was chair, he was on the faculty there in the social sciences department. Swan and Ray Wright were big backers. There was Mary Hall, Doug Hall's wife, and a woman named Mary Shaw. She was a graduate of Oxford. Boy, did everybody swoon over her because she had this great English accent! They were very representative of good, educated people, but they did get on my nerves. A lot of talking about stuff, strategy, but I was more of a doer. I felt like we needed more labor people to get out and do stuff.

I know what some people thought about me running, but I'll tell you this right now: I have never been a token in my life! I didn't care if I didn't come out of the education business. I was a hell of a lot smarter about economics and politics than the people who looked down their nose at me. We're a people used to being used as tokens; you always have to have a mouthpiece, you never thought for yourself. But in my family, the big thing was not only being able to read and write, but to think for yourself. Hubert liked that about me.

I did pick up a skill during the whole election thing—talking a lot, talking an issue to death. I would repeat things so often that some-times I thought it sounded like it came out of Hitler's book *Mein Kampf*, where he says if you say it over and over again people would be-lieve it. Of course, Hitler was talking to them about eliminating Jews!

We thought that my race, meaning my color, might show up in the vote totals, but I didn't think too hard about it. I was dealing with such basic things. And getting labor's endorsement was like getting elected. There were mostly white sections of Minneapolis that didn't vote for me—large sections in northeast Minneapolis—but other sec-tions of northeast went for me ten to one. The only thing I can think of was, in the two sections where my vote wasn't very strong, there were a lot of newly immigrated Italian and Polish people, so they might have been against me due to ignorance.

Where I did well came from hard work—campaigning house-to-house. No one ever called me names. I went into areas where women were working, whether in the home or not, and I knew how to get their vote! Of course, the women working outside the home knew I was a working woman. For the ones at home, well, northeast Minneapolis was full of kids, and I talked about the wages that their husbands should be making.

Anyway, I won the race by twenty thousand votes—I was walking on air when that happened! I couldn't go to work the next day. I took the day off and went in the next day, and if you know me, you know missing work is a very big deal.

I served six years on the library board. The day after I went on the board, I had a meeting. I wanted to know why the administration didn't have any blacks working at the library. At the time, there were lots of people in the police and the mail, but no one in the fire department or the library.

As for the library folks, I just went and talked with someone there in the personnel department, talked about the lack of black employment, and before I knew it, we had black people working there! We had two unions within the library, but these unions hadn't gotten around to getting blacks in. It was up to the City Council if the library board did nothing, and the top policy makers in the city should've done what I did if they knew the library didn't hire. The unions also have the power to advocate or persuade, but they hadn't done it. They hadn't had anybody the likes of me at that point.

That head librarian who wrote the nasty letter about me? He left before I got on the board. The system of Cleveland hired him as a librarian, so we were rid of him almost overnight. I could have been a factor in him getting out. I'm sure he had some visions of where in the world this nigger woman was going to come from!

I wouldn't run again after my last term, which ended in 1951. I was getting so deep into the union, working on pension, health, and welfare programs. I felt I could have run for school board, and maybe for Congress, but I was practically working day and night and it was tiring.

To me, it was just too hard to be out there pounding pavement in the hopes of getting into Congress. I still needed to eat, and have a roof over my head! Sure, a congressman doesn't need to worry about those things, but who was going to guarantee me I was going to be elected? North of Forest Lake, I would have to work like hell and convince people I was close to an angel, right next to God, if they were to vote for a black person.

I didn't run partly because I read reality. Yes, it was frustrating—I know how my dad must have felt when he thought about moving up electorally—but ultimately it did not hurt that much because reality set in and helped me over the hurdles.

I spent a lot of time convincing people about unions, the philosophy of workers, to recruit them. I'd talk about pensions, health programs, buying them coffee and brainwashing them! That was real stuff, closer to the people, and that's what I liked.

For the bigger offices, I would get involved in campaigns. The next person I really went to work for was Bob Latz, the son of Rubin Latz, an attorney deciding to run for the legislature. I was shooting for a state Fair Employment Practices Act, to outlaw discrimination in hiring throughout Minnesota.

Rubin was a business agent for the laundry workers on the northeast side, one of my labor mentors who was a member of the Central Labor Body. We ran for library board together, but I won the primary election, and he didn't. You've got to remember, I still was a new entity, young at the time, only forty.

During that election, he was very kind to me, walking me up and down the halls of labor temples that he knew better than I did. One thing I give him credit for is building a bridge between blacks and Jews in labor. After all, the Labor Lyceum, a Jewish labor group in the Jewish community, was the first group to endorse me. The Workman's Circle, an all-Jewish group, they raised some money for me from the Jewish business community.

I thought about the congressional seat, but that was the seat that Roy Wier wanted. He was a pretty gruff guy, able to spit tobacco anywhere, while I was a pretty clean person. He was a redneck—just shy of being a racist, I thought at first. He believed every person deserved a job, in an economic organization—his organization, the CLU! I think he was influenced by the construction trades—they would often put up every obstacle to why a black man should not be a carpenter, because they were mostly white men and they wanted their buddies to have an easier chance at jobs. But Roy realized that to save labor, he had to advocate equality across the board.

What really turned me around about him was that he desperately wanted to get on Congressman Adam Clayton Powell's labor committee. I remember at an NAACP meeting in New York in the forties, here was Powell, a powerful black man in his sixties, telling me in my forties, "Nellie, we need your boy in Congress!" That was funny, given what I had thought of him. Roy did get on. He needed support from Clarence Mitchell—he was the legislative chairman from the NAACP—to get on Powell's committee, as well as labor's, and he got it.

You see, Roy's congressional district, the third, then contained all of north Minneapolis, thick with people of color and union people, and went all the way up to North Branch, in the country. I helped Roy get in because I looked that situation over and said there were enough working-class people to pick that district up. I was skittish of places like Golden Valley—I was skeptical that there were too many traditional WASPs that would come out and bite me! And even Robbinsdale, where the KKK had meetings. Who knows why they met there, but to a person like myself, it was enough to scare me half to death!

What I did was what I also do: I just delivered votes. One area specifically that I remember so well—because the DFL leadership of this town is now trying to destroy it—is the so-called projects, now the Hollman projects area. I delivered Roy ninety-seven percent of the vote! He never did stop talking about that. I just did it because the people there knew I was into politics, and I was on the street all the time, as part of labor or the NAACP, educating and talking all the time.

For people who tell me about the demise of politics, I tell them to drop dead. Get all the poor people out there to vote. That's what I did, election after election. Work the grass roots, talk to people one on one. There are so many people who are working class or poor. That's why Republicans are running scared right now—if those people ever show up at the polls.

— Chapter 14 —

Hubert and the Dawn of Civil Rights

The only thing that I ever worked in a little opposition to Hubert on was changing to the Progressive Party when Hubert first ran for the Senate in 1948. I still worked for Hubert, day and night, as a DFL person, but nationally, I joined Henry Wallace's Progressive Party because the Progressives were going on about education for all. Here it was, an election four years after the merger, and I bolted for the third party again!

The reason why is that the Progressives were going to register black voters in the South and the national Democrats weren't going to do that. The Progressives already had an apparatus set up to get people to vote in the South. I had sweated a little bit of blood already for national black voter registration within the DFL, but people there were more taken with Hubert and the battle at home.

The Progressives were sort of like the old Farmer-Labor Party on the national scene; and in Minnesota, they were the extraprogressive people in the DFL. They got the policy and were often the people who would get the real footwork done.

I don't think it's hard to understand what I did. If you have a contingency of people who wholeheartedly believe in total equality, and are talking about getting out the vote, you'd go with them! We were going to send money and people from here to the South, and we wound up organizing all over the country, in Texas, Georgia, Mississippi.

I went to Texas. It was OK down there, I didn't have to worry about those KKK types and the like because I worked in and around the longshoremen, where as a union person, I had a lot of support. There were a lot of blacks in the longshoremen's union.

I wasn't really too worried about swinging the election to the Republicans. I wasn't really *for* Wallace per se—sometimes people, including some in labor, have trouble understanding strategy. I wanted equal opportunity voters, and if they voted for Wallace, great, but mostly, they voted. I wasn't too hung up on Truman myself—I knew the system out there, and the limits he could go to on employment and education, with the Southern Democrats, and him being a border Democrat himself. But I'll tell you what: when I got into that voting booth, even with all the work I did for the Progressives, I voted for Truman. *That's* strategy.

The group I joined was formed around the University of Minnesota. There was a professor, Dr. John Steefel, and his wife, Genevieve. She was very active in education in town, and she ran for the top position within the framework of the local Progressive Party. I wanted that position but I knew I couldn't win. So I said I wanted to be an alternate to Mrs. Steefel, the number two person.

Her winning was just not a question in a community where their reputations were so large and prestigious. I knew how people were thinking: it was OK to put me on the library board, or maybe put me in charge of working the third congressional district in north Minneapolis, where there were lots of black voters, but not in charge of a major state part of a national campaign. Even the Progressives didn't see too straight when racism and classism set in.

I was getting ready for the legislative push for a statewide Fair Employment Practices Act. I had wanted a Fair Employment Practices Commission for the City of Minneapolis, and in 1947, helped bring the ordinance through during my election to the library board. "I worked at [passing it] and I attended all of the council meetings, and sat there and listened to city attorneys lie and tell half-truths and a whole lot of things, you know. It was awful" (MHS, 21). But it passed, and for the first time there were laws preventing discrimination in hiring for women and blacks. But we needed it across the state, and I wanted those Progressives in my working coalition.

Unfortunately, those coalitions didn't always hold up very well. The Progressives were just about all of what had been left-wing DFLers, and they did support us down the line, but some farmers in the DFL, they would come together with us about family farm issues, but on employment, oftentimes not. There was a lot of convincing to do.

Sometimes it was just plain ignorance or fear about blacks. Those people that we as a family worked around, in Hinckley and Pine City, or Lakeville, these people knew Dad and knew what he had done. There were times I thought I could, like George W. Bush right now, just ride in on my father's coattails.

Again, there was not too much real hard opposition; usually someone in their family had given them an argument that they would have to hire blacks on the farm, or that they might have tougher times getting jobs. These were not all, or even most farmers in the DFL. You always had to go back to the rights of the family farmer, making sure they could stand up to the power of the middleman and the corporation, to try to make the point how similar power could hurt people in the black community by discrimination.

Hubert, like me, was very into grassroots politics, so he understood me going with the Progressives on the presidential ballot. He knew not to oppose me on something so basic as registering more voters.

I'll tell you what—had we gone in there on a national ballot with Hubert Humphrey for king of the United States, we would have gotten ninety-nine percent of the black vote and a whole lot of new black voters. After Hubert's speech to the 1948 Democratic National Convention about the Democrats leaving behind states' rights and taking the country into the bright sunshine of human rights, I was going back and forth to New York to work with a national caucus for the Hotel and Restaurant workers. This was strictly a civil and human rights caucus, about a hundred and fifty people who believed in equal opportunity. Well, after talking to blacks there, I know the lowest black person all over the country was ready to vote for Hubert a dozen times!

That speech forced people to say, if I've got any intelligence, I've got to treat people a different way. There was a change all over the state. The thing I liked about it was that it hit people to the point where they would write it down and talk about it. Prior to that, talking about equal opportunity seemed to get caught in their throat. People began to take a new look all over the country.

I was in Minneapolis when this all happened. Of course, I wasn't going to be caucusing with the national Democrats that year! I went out to Philadelphia for the Progressive Party's meeting. The reaction there to Humphrey's speech was no different than other people in the North. I stayed close to several ministers in town, to see what issues they talked about to their constituency, and whether the reaction was good, bad, or indifferent. They were saying he's a great man.

Later on, I spoke in several of the churches on several things he spoke on; I always punctuated my talks with references to education. Hubert legitimized me in the white political community, and I know in the black community I legitimized him. I guess the closest thing to advice I ever gave him about that talk was what I always told him in general: not to dress it up in political and racial dressing, say that it's just the right thing to do. That's what's wrong with feminism sometimes—they dress it up as something to fix things for white, upper-class women, rather than just it's the right thing to do!

Some people talk me up as the mentor of Humphrey on civil rights. We talked a lot about civil and human rights. Those were the two issues that he and I talked about constantly, along with a good, general qualified education.

What I think I taught him was that there was somebody else out there in the community. There was a very negative picture—in fact, still is—about blacks in work and community and education and being responsible. I think some of the *most* responsible people came out of the black community!

The national Democrats were not very good on race then. Hubert's total concept was equality, of course. His problem was how to maintain power to become a senator of the United States when some of his national party's friends were on the other side, not wanting to give the black community the right to vote. It was so hard for me to come in contact with people like that. These Southern Democrats thought if you were black, you shouldn't even live! And there were plenty of them at the 1948 convention.

I was not against the DFL, though in some of my naiveness, I did not realize how it would go over in the party. In the next election in Minnesota, the state DFL committee wanted to discipline me, for being with the Progressives, at the convention when I tried to be seated as a delegate. Orville Freeman was leading one of those charges not to seat me as a delegate:

> He was chairing a meeting and he found every excuse under the sun why he couldn't seat me. Hubert was flying back from Washington and he came in and Orville even had his lunch so he could eat on the platform, [during the] meeting. I saw him and Hubert talking, and when we opened up the meeting again Hubert just stood up. The first thing he said, "Nellie Stone has just been seated as a delegate!" (MHS, 40)

Humphrey, Freeman, Walter Mondale—they're far from being the same guy. Hubert was far and away the best intellectually, and as a humanitarian. I never thought I'd meet anyone who could compare until I got to Walter Mondale. He's a very low key person, but very exact and to the point.

Orville tried to carry out the platform. I don't remember any speeches he ever made. Orville was not quite the spellbinder or anything like that on policy, a human policy, like Hubert was. [Freeman, a staunch member of the DFL's anticommunist wing, organized an intraparty campaign to rid the party of reds. He was helped by a young organizer named Walter Mondale, who had orchestrated a similar purge in the Young DFL in 1947. Freeman went on to become governor of Minnesota for three consecutive terms in the 1950s and was secretary of agriculture under both John Kennedy and Lyndon Johnson.]

Hubert Humphrey was the key person on things such as breaking down racism in the military. Truman was a person who was there on civil rights, issuing the antidiscrimination orders, but Hubert Humphrey was the key person getting it all going.

Later in the 1950s, I was involved in the National Armed Services Against Racism—the air force, the navy, and the army. Truman only fully desegregated the armed services after we campaigned on it.

The first thing we did when we were campaigning against military racism was go to Walter White, the head of the NAACP—the best we ever had—and he notified Hubert in Washington. We sent a delegation from Minneapolis: William Craddock, the president of the NAACP here, Jonas Schwartz, the chair of the legal redress committee. I didn't go on the trip, but I stirred up all the trouble!

I'm the one that made the motion that the Minneapolis branch of the NAACP pick up on military racism. I did it because there was just no action anyplace. As much as you want total equality right away, you can't get that. But when certain things open up, certain dialogue about issues, if you have any sense at all, you jump off.

World War Two is a good example. I heard some percentages, that a large percent of the field casualties at one point during World War Two were black. In Vietnam it would be even worse. As an activist you try to stay on top and emotional with your constituency, and this was on their minds. I knew the black veterans had served long and well in World War Two, but there were still some parts of the service closed to us. I was reading about it all the time in the people-of-color press. I'm sad to say labor was reflecting the general public out there on the total issue of discrimination. Labor was a hundred and ten percent behind getting rid of it—about ten years later.

The Minneapolis branch wasn't too large at the time. I told one of the lawyers on the committee that he never got off his you-know-what to vote for the motion. He said, "Oh, Nellie, we're not that big for a national campaign, we've only got six hunded people." But size never mattered to me. The job had to be done, and what difference does it make if there are six hundred people or a thousand people in the Minneapolis chapter of the NAACP? I found out I can do some of my strongest organizing with five people—if they are working hard, say, for unions, and rights of people of color and women.

We educated people locally, then we got the delegation to lobby Congress and the president. We sent five people, but Hubert worked those congressmen after we left. As I said, five people can change things if they're aimed right and work hard.

Chapter 15

Nellie and Thurgood Marshall

In 1949, there was this big argument at the national NAACP convention in Los Angeles, where black labor—and I really want to identify black labor because they were so far ahead of the black community it wasn't even funny—wanted to do something big about integration. We were pushing the NAACP to take on a case that became *Brown versus the Board of Education*. That was the one that upset separate versus equal education for black kids and brought in integration.

This was in 1949, what I'm talking about, not 1954, when the case was decided. Back then, Thurgood Marshall, who was our NAACP lawyer, was not inclined to take the case. See, I know Thurgood in a way most feminists and other liberals don't. Thurgood followed the educated part of the black community and the churches. They were more middle class, and not economically or politically inclined to do something as radical as go to court over integration.

The big thing that happened in L.A. was labor versus the elite. We in labor outvoted the other side and the NAACP went to take on *Brown versus the Board*. Most people in the so-called black community—even the late Jonas Schwartz, who headed up the legal redress committee for the NAACP in Minneapolis—didn't see this coming. Jonas wasn't that close to labor. We wanted hard action and some teeth into whatever legislation got passed about this. The intellectual blacks and Jews, they seemed to want this committee and that committee, to negotiate here and there.

Jonas's position was the milquetoast position, the path of least resistance. You could go on forever with a negotiation or an individual case before a discriminated-against person got a job. I just went on and on. There were a lot of luncheons and dinner meetings—talk, talk, talk. I remember one night a few years before this in Minneapolis at a meeting, I said, here we are, talking about public accommodations, making it easier for black people to stay in a hotel, or eat in a restaurant, but what about a guarantee in employment, so that anyone in the black community can have the money to stay in that hotel room? I felt the same way about education helping people get the money that was needed.

Now many of us radicals, the people in labor, wanted to make outlawing segregation plain law—you just can't discriminate in education. At first, even I was against going to court because I favored putting it into law. Before I got to Los Angeles, I decided supporting a court case was a good way to go, to at least get my foot in the door.

They didn't allow the rank-and-file labor people into one meeting during the NAACP convention—it was just supposed to be all the legal people. I got in anyway. What happened is that Charles Howard, a black lawyer from Des Moines, had made a nominating speech for Henry Wallace the year before, so we were friends from the Progressives. He got me into the lawyers' meeting, where I wasn't exactly supposed to be. That's how I got to hear Thurgood sound off. There were lawyers, both black and white, who thought they knew more about what the black community wanted than ourselves.

The two of us that Charley Howard got in were me and Jimmy Hicks, who came out of the top black press, in Baltimore, an African-American paper. He and I had formed quite a bond over black issues, and the white media, especially the Associated Press, was very influenced by Jimmy's work. What happened is he would lead all of the Eastern press philosophically. He wrote for all the big black newspapers up and down the eastern seaboard. Jimmy had no problem understanding how to write about basic civil rights and the right to eat and work. Few writers writing about economic matters today could possibly touch Jimmy Hicks. He was such a tremendous writer.

About the only difference between Jimmy and me was that he liked scotch and I liked brandy, so when we went into seclusion to plot, we had to get two bottles.

In this lawyers-only meeting, there was an old judge, a white man out of North Carolina or South Carolina who brought down a lot of opposition on Thurgood's head. This man was a federal judge, and I'm sorry, I just can't remember his name. He was one of the few people in the South who supported civil rights, one of the few people who told Thurgood Marshall he was too complacent. He just pitched a fit, said blacks really have to read and write to get a job to feed themselves—he was just down to earth, and you know I went all out because he was talking my language.

This is the argument against Thurgood Marshall. Thurgood had started out with *Plessy versus Ferguson,* the Supreme Court decision from several decades back that said blacks could be separate but equal. Thurgood was still arguing that blacks should go for more educational resources on the basis of separate but equal. The old judge just turned him around. The basis behind the old judge, my feeling was, was that he was a constitutional lawyer.

Of course, we were giving Thurgood opposition, too; in the convention we were known as the Young Turks. About a third of the [NAACP] convention was longshoremen or labor people, who were more radical. There was contempt for us being young, arguing with these hallowed people. "But that person is out of Harvard, that great institution . . ." But we had the votes to make things go our way.

I saw Thurgood at all the national conventions, including many before he became the first black justice of the Supreme Court. Even in Los Angeles, despite disagreements, we could talk, say hello, and even got to be friends. I remember one convention in Atlantic City, I was going up the escalator, and he was coming down, and we met in the middle at the same time and decided to both get off so we could talk. We talked about issues pertinent to the black community, and tried to get to know each other better. He got to know that people like me were the power in the NAACP—Thurgood could get sidetracked with all the middle class. But he knew that the working people and labor were the power then. When we called for a black caucus for labor in Atlantic City, a third of the people went to caucus.

He and I agreed mostly; he also couldn't disagree with me too loudly then because he worked for the NAACP and I was on the Minneapolis board when we were one of the most outstanding branches in the U.S. Too bad so much of our reputation was lost when too many people wanted to associate themselves with the white middle class. That happened shortly in 1952, 1953. There were lots of middle-class people who did not want to be part of fund-raising to send labor people like me to NAACP meetings, even if we were elected to go.

I know you hear me criticize the middle class a lot. I generally don't like any reference to the middle, because that sounds like weakness to me. I don't see why there should ever be a compromise on things that are basically humane. Sure, you have to wait for the right time on issues, but the middle class wants to slow things down too much, and they're not the ones paying the price.

Plus, the middle-class people came to fear labor. I think it's because labor was pictured by the big press as being radical and associated with the Mafia, even though unions were trying to help the very people who were being discriminated against.

The way I saw it, the only strength that sprung to the fore was taking care of each other, humanity, and the labor movement was the only vehicle to do that—certainly it was the best organization economically for blacks. I think that's historically very evident, considering the size of the labor movement coming out of the depression. And besides, I think most good ideas start out as radical ideas—look at civil rights. Any organization that wants to change from the status quo is considered radical.

Thurgood got to be a very good judge. He happened to be in the right place and time to be appointed, by President Johnson—right in the heart of Johnson's Great Society, which was coming out of the New Deal. Thurgood was with that right on down the line.

People who lobbied to get him on the Supreme Court knew he

learned the basic concepts. There were people from Minnesota, Ohio, New York—me and Hubert and senators from those states lobbied for him.

Of course, you can't lobby the Supreme Court, but you can lobby the Senate and Congress who can ride herd on the president on who he supports for the Court. I tell you, it wouldn't have bothered me to lobby the Supreme Court, though. I knew a couple of other Supreme Court justices pretty well. [Former Chief Justice Warren] Burger I knew. Did we get along? Well, we didn't hit each other.

— Chapter 16 —

Seamstress

In 1950, the Athletic Club fired me again. The receptionist's job was the last one they fired me from. I had taken advantage of the desk and telephone for union stuff. They said I couldn't do that. I always had an argument—how else was I supposed to get organizing? They used *their* phones to organize for the Chamber of Commerce—I was just using their model against them!

I got wind when they started to say I couldn't take time off for my politics unless I paid somebody to work my shift. I was on such boards as the library board—can you imagine penalizing me for being an elected official? There was another woman on the board whose employer gave her time off! That was the first sense I had that they were getting tough with me. They used that "work insubordination"—a wonderful word, if you're a boss.

They were able to fire me despite our union contract because they could fire anybody as far as that was concerned. You had the right to meetings, and arbitrators, but that doesn't stop the initial firing of people.

When I got to arbitration in 1950, I didn't want my damn job back. I wanted more skills in political organizing, and wanted to know more about the contract negotiations. Even though I didn't work there, I maintained my office as the vice president of Local 665. I figured I could find a place to work that would let me be an elected official and a union person.

The obvious thing to me was I was becoming a pretty skilled person, not just organizing but in dressmaking and alterations. I sewed from the time I was nine. All I wanted was a job. But the places I went to go see said I needed experience in a shop. I said, well, how do I get it?

When I owned my own sewing shop years later, the way people who worked for me came to me was not because of any indication of a shared ethnic background. It was purely and simply a lack of experience—other businesses wouldn't hire them because they had no experience. Well, if you're not hired in the first place, how are you supposed to get the experience? That's how they all ruled out hiring people of color. It was hard for me to take—a lot of these businesses were Jewish-owned, and I was under the assumption that blacks and Jews didn't discriminate. Because of our parents we'd all been discriminated against, so I thought we were too intellectual to discriminate against each other.

The thing is, it almost makes me reluctant to tell the story because you hate to see anyone be discriminated against. I never discriminated against anyone in my life—you'd think I was the only one. My family made the connection between blacks and Jews, Jews and blacks. We'd shared that ghetto situation in our history.

Lots of places turned me down. For a time, I did straight sewing in a big dress factory. But I wanted more specialized skills than a small shop could bring. Finally, I got my experience sewing at a smaller shop, the Wilson Alteration Shirt Shop right here on First Avenue North. I remember a test, sewing two raggedy pieces together—you needed to show the ability to sew a straight seam.

Why did they give me the chance? I think their eye was too set on production to discriminate. You've got to get production out of a small shop, it's as simple as that. You've got to work harder to compete with the big guns.

I noticed something when I first started: the wife of the man who owned the business, Hilda Wilson, she liked to sew herself, but she was very slow. She was fumbling with an alteration. I said, let me sew that, I won't charge you. You have to use more vision and imagination when you alter something than with straight sewing.

I hated to see Hilda wear some of what she did. She was not a bad-looking woman, and I'd fix her clothes. There was a method to my madness: I wanted to get away from routine work.

I also wanted that experience using their machines. I didn't quite know the setup for Wilsons', but when they said shirts, I knew it was one of the toughest construction jobs in sewing, and I wanted to know those hard things. I was learning about their business all the time. I recognized that if I was going to open my own shop, it would be pretty much the same. My working there was good for both of us. I kept theirs almost the best small business in town. My production was fifty shirts a day, which was darn good.

I was doing alterations only. Typically, shortening sleeves or putting new collars on old shirts, which is one of the toughest jobs in the sewing field. If you get one stitch off kilter, the collar won't attach or look right with the points coming down just so. We also did cuffs, same thing. It's hard because there's the tedious work to it, very exact work.

I was good at the mechanical side—I could put any Ford car up on blocks and work on it, so I could handle sewing machines. There were a lot of women working at these places, but also quite a few men because there were so many machines that needed to be kept running.

They had jump-basters, heavy topstitchers for men's suits and topcoats. At the time, I had the experience of making anything I wanted to, but not the experience on a commercial-special machine like the jump-basters. I could make men's denim shirts and overalls pretty good. That's what I started out doing on the farm—my dad would buy an amount of denim and chambray for me and my grandma. She didn't sew as much because she was busy cooking and taking care of babies.

At this time, I also did do some night work with a company called Zero King. Those were some of the early snowsuits. I did the whole garment there.

There was a lot of difference between being an employee at Wilson's and being one at the Athletic Club. Wilsons' was a family-type business and did all of their own work. The management wasn't hard on me there because they were just like me; theirs was a very intellectual way of running the business. They were a very small mom-and-pop business that wanted to make money, and when they got a good person, they treated them right. We worked eight hours a day, that was it. They had no illusions about who was better than anyone else. That was very nice. There were three of us girls who worked for them the same. I was at a machine right next to Hilda herself. The management was right there with us, and we were out of each other's way most of the time.

I didn't go after a job in politics. By that time, I knew where the rough spots were, who I would have to knock down to even get an endorsement from the DFL Party to run for something bigger. I really didn't want to be a staff person, because I knew what staff people had to do. If you worked for a senator or a congressman, you spent half your time raising money and half your time doing social work. I was already doing a lot of social-work-type stuff. If I had a paid political job I'd open myself to all the pettiness from everybody else who wanted the job, including green-eyed women who wanted to take jobs away from any woman who had gotten one.

— *Chapter 17* —

Red-Baiting

I knew that after the DFL merger some Democrats would try to throw us on the dung heap because we were radicals. I've always said you have to be radical to change things in this country. That's been called socialism, or even communism.

By the late 1940s, early 1950s, the fighting about Communists became a bigger deal. It was hard for some people to get seated at party conventions, because Hubert was on a red binge at the time. Hubert lost a little bit of his clout with us. It was just one of those things. It wasn't so much what Hubert said, but there were people to say it for him—young people who couldn't find their way across the bathroom. They'd say, "Oh that's a Communist over there." Hubert could have stopped these young men, but he didn't, and that's what we blamed him for.

Hubert had to prove he was tough on the reds. The Russians were our enemies. Some of the people who were very good advisers to Hubert were also kind of brainwashed. They thought that everything we did in the labor movement was very radical, that the Communists or extreme socialists were responsible for bad things, a loss of freedom.

Don't lump all the Communists together here. I had been part of the Young Communist League, a younger group of people who stood for education and equal opportunity for all. I wasn't a Joe Stalin Communist, I wasn't going to take anyone's freedom away, not at all, and I never heard any young Communist say anything like that.

I never got caught up in red-baiting. I knew it was the wrong thing to do, but to be honest, Hubert and I skirted around it. We never balled up our fists at each other, and I didn't have any discussions with him about what was going on. He knew where I was coming from. I think he had to placate some of the national Democrats. He really was a good person in between. I guess if you make progress, you don't kill off the main person. That's a part of politics. You don't have to compromise all the time, but we had hard legislation to get passed, be it a city ordinance for equal opportunity, or one at the state level.

Red-baiting created divisions between blacks and Jews. The enemy of both wanted to put something in the mind of the other. Part of what the conservatives, the establishment, was saying was that the Jews were Communists and the blacks should stay away. That was how they wanted to split the labor coalition.

I remember a meeting, I just got so angry that I jumped out of my seat! They would say, that's a communist idea, that's what the Communists are saying. What we were talking about was education for all, equality for people of color. I kept asking, "Why should the Communists get all the credit for the good ideas! Why should the Communists get the benefit of promoting opportunity for people?"

> Mr. [Cecil] Newman said, "You know, I'm getting so sick and tired of hearing that kind of reference to people. Anybody in the black community that's 45 or older, if they haven't rubbed arms with communism, there's something wrong with them!" And I never forgot that because it was so real, you know. If you hadn't rubbed elbows with the Left, you know, what are you about? (MHS, 44)

Look, history shows this: unless the left wing begins to assert itself politically, there won't be any good education. You have to just move forward. Stop and think of the education that people in Russia get, especially what women got. What's bad about that? We were behind! When they sent up that woman and that dog into space we got scared because we knew we were behind them educationally.

I was told people were kicked out of the DFL Party, but I don't remember precisely. I know a lot of people had a hard time. If they got red-baited enough, they just didn't come around, and you didn't have the benefit of their arguments on various issues.

I had powerful people looking out for me sometimes, such as the late Charlie Horn, president and owner of Federated Cartridge. They named the Horn Towers public housing project in south Minneapolis after him. He was a friend of Roosevelt, the Curt Carlson of his day, and he liked the things I was doing for the community. He was what I would call an entrepreneur of people. He hired Cecil Newman to hire on an equal opportunity basis for Federated Cartridge. [In the 1940's, Federated Cartridge employed twenty percent of Minnesota's adult black population.] Cecil used to kid me that Charlie didn't like everybody, he was particular of who he liked. The joke was, here I was a radical, and Charlie liked me.

Right after World War Two, I turned down a job at the Federal Court that Charlie Horn tried to get me. He came after me. He said, "I don't like your radicalism, but I like you!"

As radical as I was, I cleared the way at the FBI and the CIA with his help. He said, "I'll fight all the way for you." He told me later he never worked so hard to get someone cleared. He was trying to tell me how hard he worked, but I could top him! I told him he'd never worked to get someone a pension plan!

I wanted to stay in the union, to keep organizing. Working for a union pension plan was part of why I didn't want to change jobs at that time. I was such an animal—I was already where I wanted to be. I was close to Hubert. I was involved in politics.

In 1946, with red-baiting gathering steam, Nellie was a featured speaker at the Twenty-second Anniversary Lenin Memorial Meeting, a benefit to raise money for striking union workers. The very public embrace of Communist beliefs by the newly elected library board member had consequences.

I think it was George Matthews, he was [an alderman] at that time, who said, "Nellie, what in the world did you allow yourself to be used in a meeting like that for?" And he went on to say what the repercussions would be politically. I told him, George, you forget what we stand for, what I stand for, and I'm just seeing a furtherance of that in meetings like this, especially with [a strike] coming up. (MHS, 40)

Nellie Stone, Left-Winger, Defeated in Union Election

Nellie Stone, a member of the Minneapolis library board and for many years a leftwing figure in Minneapolis labor circles, has been defeated for re-election in her own union.... Mrs. Stone lost 351 to 199 to Eddie Larson in the race for vice president of Local 665, Hotel and Restaurant Workers union.... Defeat of Mrs. Stone marks the final step in ridding the local of leftwing officers who at one time exercised virtual control in the union.

Minneapolis Morning Tribune, February 7, 1950

Nellie Stone Letter Confirms Her Break With Leftist Parties

Nellie Stone, 909 Girard Ave. No., member of the Minneapolis Library Board and active in the labor union movement, in a letter to "Fellow workers and friends" dated February 26, announced she had "severed my relationships with the Progressive and Communist parties." . . .

"After many months of thought and because of the present world crisis, I feel obligated to my friends and fellow workers to inform them of my present political status and beliefs. . . .

"At this time, I am not affiliated with any political party. I have severed my relationships with the Communist and Progressive parties. . . .

"My mind is still the same about the needs of workers, the most oppressed people in our society. For a long period of time I have had certain disagreements with the programs of the parties named above.

"I was more than a little disturbed by policies which run counter to the needs of all workers and similarly policies which are diametrically opposed to the interests of the Negro and other minority people.

"I have studied these contradictions and have come to the conclusion that I can serve the workers cause best by announcing my disaffiliation from these parties. . . .

"I want to say to all of you that I still stand for a real workers party."

Minneapolis Morning Tribune, March 2, 1951

I wanted to get everybody off my back was basically it. As I said, there was some misunderstanding of my association with the Young Communist League, compared to the parent organization of the Communist Party, and too many people thought they were the same.

I was on my way back to the DFL Party, though I had never really left. Most people are not used to black people doing that kind of sophisticated politics that I was trying to do in getting rid of those party labels. Everybody thinks you are red, you're subversive.

My association and philosophical belief with those parties, the belief within me, was true, but my bottom line was always about jobs and education. I was getting a lot of questions—a lot of people don't understand the black and Native American communities, how you have to run under those obstacles to get to point A, let alone to B and C, where you want to go politically.

Eddie Larsen was someone that the conservative white establishment put up against me. This was part of the effort to brainwash blacks and Jews against radicals. I understood that those union people who voted against me were smart! Because they wanted to eat and feed their families, and get a good education.

I just took my loss in stride, as they say. I knew I was going to keep in politics, and I would be a power in certain areas. I stayed on in my powerful positions in the local, too.

Six months after Nellie's leftist affiliations made headlines, she was one of six Minneapolitans honored by the city's Chamber of Commerce for distinguished public service.

That was for the great things I had done while on the library board, because I had always hammered away at the concepts of equal opportunity and education for all. I thought that award was not quite fair to the other people, from other organizations, who had done right promoting those issues too. But the fact is, that was my philosophy, not any crazy label they tried to stick me with.

The red-hunters in Washington, they didn't get around to me until I was interviewed by government agents in the fifties. Being older, almost fifty, and deeper into politics, I was thinking that what was going on in Washington wasn't very good, but they probably didn't bother me because ol' Joe McCarthy and the rest had bigger fish to go after.

Finally, a local FBI person called me. He was very polite—we made an appointment to get together. When we met, he asked me about a St. Paul woman who worked at Fort Snelling, a black woman. Her husband was very active in radical politics. As I remember it there were two guys interviewing me that day.

I said to one, why worry about her? Are you worried she's going to contaminate the pots and pans she's washing out there? What could she do with pots and pans to contaminate people's minds? They kind of sneered at me, but they never threatened me with jail. Whatever thought I put into jail at that time wasn't worth much.

Then they went so far as to take me before a federal grand jury. They told me that they thought I was advocating radical education—they never did spell that one out. I asked Doug Hall, who was a civil rights attorney as well as our labor lawyer, to come with me, but they wouldn't let anyone in but me. To a grand jury!

The man who questioned me, I think his name was Howard Gelb. Here's the crazy thing: his mother lived near me on Girard Avenue North. I used to solicit up and down our block for Dollars for Democrats—that was my real toehold into the Democratic Party. You know, a dollar a month for Democrats. We raised a lot of money that way. Now it's a dollar a week.

Gelb was—what do you call it?—the chair, the legal chair of the federal grand jury. The prosecutor, that's it. And the fact that he knew me made him go easy.

He was concerned about the Young Communist League because obviously they were into communism. One question was, did you know people in the Young Communist League or a communist organization?

So I asked him a question back. I said, "Mr. Gelb"—I was very nice—I said, "are you asking me whose membership card I had ever seen?" And he said yes.

I said, "I can truthfully tell you, nobody's but mine." And that was the end of that. I was not about to incriminate anybody at that time. I was beginning to see what they were doing to people they identified as members of the Communist Party. Bill Sennett from the Teamsters union was locked up for years and years. I raised dollars for him while he was in jail. He was there just for union organizing, basically. There's a whole history of people like this—people like Tom Mooney, he came out of the mines in Wyoming and Montana.

Telling that story just now, I made it sound pretty easy, but I don't think I slept the night before the questioning, thinking, What simple thing can I do so I won't belch out anything? That was the question I came up with: had I seen anyone's membership cards? I truthfully hadn't.

— Chapter 18 —

Fair Employment and Housing

Some things you remember precisely. I remember April 15, 1955, the day fair employment became law in Minnesota. I remember because I was so tired I could hardly hold up. In '55, I worked all over the state, and then spent the final push working the legislature. I felt like I could sleep for two months, but I didn't because we had to get to work on the Fair Housing Act, which passed five years later, in 1960.

There was a lot of belief on the part of the legislature at that time in reverse discrimination—that was where they started that baloney. Some of the legislators would tell me that this law would mean whites would lose jobs, and I said, how could it be *reverse* discrimination when it wasn't fair in the first place? If there's no power or authority for the people you're lobbying for, and you want to talk reverse discrimination, it's not a valid argument. At that point, what do you have to discriminate with?

I don't care who you are, or where you grew up, racism was circulating around. I had a niece-in-law, Judy Patterson, who is white. My blood niece, Diane Patterson, Judy's sister-in-law, is a mixed-race person. Judy went to work for Minnegasco in the old Kresge Building. Judy tried to see if she could get a job for Diane, her mixed-race sister-in-law, but her bosses didn't ever give her any concrete answer.

That's the difference in people. Our family, we are a good family, with the concerns of other people. We're all that way. My sister Gladys had nine children—and she fed everyone in the neighborhood, black, white, or indifferent!

When we came through in the '40s with the first draft of the Fair Employment Practices Act, I tried to get that through the NAACP and our legal redress committee at that time moved to table my motion. My goodness, the NAACP! But I went over to the Central Labor Body and got it through. . . . I went out and did some more organizing for memberships in the NAACP, lifted it off the table, and got it passed.

You remember Jonas Schwartz? I think he had decided it was reverse discrimination, that was the argument. And we had a knockdown, drag-out about that one.

In 1953, the NAACP took over the state effort. There had been a fair employment practices state council before that. I participated on the periphery of it, but the leadership was a little different and they weren't doing what they should have done, so the state conference of the NAACP decided to take on this job and we did and we passed it. (MHS, 18)

Sometimes people ask me why I care about the DFL platform so much. It's true that nobody seems to read it much anymore, but I tell you there have been times I felt as though my life depended on it, and Fair Employment is a perfect example.

I was able to argue for equality in many platform fights. I'd tell people, what good is the public education we all support without total equality. The only way to spell that message out to your allies is to put it in the platform.

We needed a lot of Republican help on Fair Employment, to get it through the legislature, and we got it. I think our best friend on that side in the legislature was Senator Al Quie, who later became governor of Minnesota. I had lobbied him very hard. Our politics didn't always agree, but he was very human. He later appointed me to the Department of Economic Security board, even though he was a Republican. If I got a Senate leader like Al Quie around to where I wanted him, he carried the conference committee, and that carried the day.

I remember that Monday before the bill passed, I went in and talked and bantered with him. He said, "You know what, Nellie, I went home over the weekend and did some plowing, and I decided to vote for your legislation." I said, "You know what, Senator Quie, I went home and cultivated too, and I almost thought I was talking to God." I wasn't trying to be facetious, but I think he was a born-again at the time, and he was saying that God talked to him. If that's what it took, that's what I did, too.

I think there's a lot to religion, even though I am one of the least believers in religion; I just believe in good and bad, just none of the myth jargon, I guess.

A lot of the Republicans were very religious, and in the best of 'em, that made them more humane. I think we had more than our share of humane Republicans here in Minnesota. I was good friends with Republicans on the bench, such as Luther Youngdahl, who was there after he was governor. Also Elmer Andersen—the good Elmer who was governor. The bad Elmer was C. Elmer Anderson, he was from Bemidji. He just went along. He never paid much attention to the humane things. The good Elmer was jumping up and down with the rest of us about Fair Housing.

A lot of the lobbying came pretty easy to me because I knew people around the state. I was on the various policy-making bodies of organizations like the DFL, my union and the state assemblies, the NAACP. They would wonder what the driving force was for me at the legislature. I showed up. I looked at their faces. I challenged them for what they didn't do right.

It would be a lovely situation if everyone could just start being not racist, but you look at that man in Texas who was dragged behind a car beaten to smithereens. It's still out there.

The Texas case made me remember way back in 1954, 1955, right around this time. There was a case in Walker, Minnesota, and the connection was that it came right around the time they lynched Emmett Till down in the South. He was abducted and killed in Mississippi for allegedly making some kind of remark to a white woman that was a typical male remark. He was killed because he did that, but really just because of the color of his skin.

This Walker case came before the local NAACP at about the same time. The Walker situation wasn't about violence, but it was a case of discrimination of a black teacher and a family from Indiana. They had reserved a cabin at one of the resorts in Walker. She was very brown-skinned. She had all the credentials, the reservation, plus her secretary where she taught school took notes on everything. The owner of the resort was Native American—the same band of Chippewa that one of my cousins belonged to, who was married to a white man. The courts ruled against the NAACP and said she didn't have to rent to the black family. I don't remember what their reasoning was, but they could do it.

After the courts ruled, we went to the Minnesota legislature, got everything thrown in but the kitchen sink. This was the start of Fair Housing getting passed after many long years of trying. To just see that blatant discrimination about people trying to stay somewhere made some people think.

On December 1, 1955, less than eight months after Minnesota's Fair Employment Act passed, Rosa Parks refused to comply with a bus driver's demand that she give up her seat for a white man on a Montgomery, Alabama, bus. Her arrest led to the Montgomery bus boycotts, one of the first expressions of collective resistance to segregation.

I didn't know too much about Rosa Parks when that happened, but I knew the man who got her a lawyer—E. D. Nixon, the agent for the Brotherhood of Sleeping Car Porters. Labor again. I knew her incident was serious when I heard it. I never had to go to the back of the bus in Minnesota, but I had been reading about these things happening in the *Chicago Defender* all my life.

Even though I thought what happened to Rosa Parks was serious, it didn't seem as significant as it turned out to be. I do remember thinking this was good politics—I had grown a long nose for politics by that time—and that she could be an example of what was going down as far as outright discrimination and the need to fight back.

In 1960 or so, when blacks started sitting in at lunch counters to protest not being served, I participated in all of those local sit-ins: Grant's, Kresge's, and Woolworth's. Every Friday and Saturday, we picketed in solidarity with the national scene. I was working in the Kresge Building at the time. Some of the people looked at me like I was kind of nuts, but I knew that what I was doing was strictly honorable. People here either supported you, or they kept their mouths shut.

I remember there was a white businessman walking the picket line—Jim Luger. He ran Luger Enterprises, and sold can openers and knives to all the department stores. He was walking the picket lines with us, and we ran into a buyer from Dayton's. He said to Jim, "The next time your order comes up, count it out."

Now, I was the person who brought in Jim Luger; he was from one of the old families in Minneapolis. He was in the Korean War, and looked me up because of my involvement in criminal and civil rights. He said his family was having a new baby every year, and he didn't want his children growing up ignorant people. That was pretty impressive. It was a good mix in those picket lines. Most of the white people were labor people who understood well what going on.

In 1957, liberal state legislators introduced the Fair Housing bill in the Minnesota legislature. The bill outlawed racial discrimination in private- or public-owned houses and apartments. One sponsor of the bill was Don Fraser of Minneapolis, who would go on to Congress and, then served a long stint as Minneapolis's mayor in the 1980s and 1990s. Even though he represented the liberal University of Minnesota district as a state representative, Fraser remembers coming under sustained attack by those who thought private citizens shouldn't have to rent or sell to blacks. The bill had powerful sponsors, including Republican state Senator Elmer L. Andersen, who would sign the bill as governor.

The Fair Housing battle is how I got hooked up with a lot of great future DFLers, people who just knew in their hearts it was the right thing to do.

One was Marty Sabo, who was later speaker of the Minnesota House and seems like he has been a Minnesota congressman forever! One day in the late '50s, George Murk, the head of the musicians union, told me, if you people—meaning the political labor people— don't knock off a state representative from over at the University of Minnesota named Carlson, you should feel bad. He's not on board for your Fair Housing bill behind the scenes.

Even though this Carlson was a labor person, I told George Murk, I'll knock him off! The Fair Housing bill was pigeonholed in commit- tee—this was '58 or '59—and we had to rely on a friend to bring it out. A woman professor I knew at Augsburg College said she had a good man over in the Seven Corners area who would support it. That turned out to be Marty Sabo. I helped him get the endorsement over this Carlson.

Don Fraser went overboard to push for Fair Housing in the Minnesota legislature, when a lot of people wouldn't. He worked with another legislator from Rochester named Sandy Keith, which is how Fair Housing later played a role in my decision in one of the bitterest endorsement fights ever, the 1966 endorsement fight between Keith and Karl Rolvaag.

It took twenty-one ballots—I took a lot of rough talk from some of my DFL friends for supporting Sandy. Rolvaag and I were good friends, and I had gone for him on many issues. But Karl supported Fair Housing only up to a point. Karl was kind of a strange person. He could not care more or less for inner-city issues, starting with educa- tion. It was hard for me to understand because Karl's father was a professor at St. Olaf for many years. There were issues on equal op- portunity for people in which he would drag his feet in mysterious ways. Was this another example of having trouble with academics?

Sandy did more than just go through the motions; he was a very bright guy, and he went out of his way to understand what the slave system did to minority people. I voted for him at the convention, but I was only an alternate.

At that convention, as you can imagine, there was plenty of time to talk. I think that was when Fritz Mondale and I first talked. Mondale was a very impressive young man, plus he was very good looking—not that that was a factor with me, because God knows I was older than that, nearly sixty at this time!

He was with the Young DFLers when I first met him. He and I went into the old Radisson Hotel in St. Paul to talk about the ramifications of the party platform—just generally what we should have in the platform. Then we started talking about the input of the Democratic National Committee. He impressed me with his direct honesty. A lot of people said Hubert was phony on this, that, or the other, but he never came off as phony. Mondale also never came off as phony.

He seemed honest in his commitment to people and certain issues, like labor and the equality of women. He was a little bit beyond a lot of people who just used the verbiage. I always felt so secure with Fritz Mondale. Humphrey, too, but [DFL governor] Orville Freeman came off a little harder. Freeman seemed like he really wanted Hubert to believe in him, but he was trying so hard I wasn't sure he really felt it in his bones. What do I mean? I wasn't easy to convince on politics; I didn't care how well they talked when I made my mind up who to support.

Walter had that air—his words were soothingly honest. His mind was like a steel trap, and he was on to the next subject with something intelligent to say before I knew it.

The point of all this is, I want to put people in office to make change, and to make *real* change, you need laws. You need everything short of taking racists to the closet and beating them within an inch of their lives! We have to have a change of heart inside everyone, sure—but I want to help the heart along with legislation.

Chapter 19

Entrepreneur

Don Fraser and this whole group came at me for a political job. I didn't want to be in a paid job, I wanted to be free to do my politics. I didn't mind having constituents—that's my strength—but to do a paid job puts you at the mercy of a lot of politicians.

The job Don wanted me to take was a national job with the Peace Corps. It was a good idea in a way—I grew up around a horse and buggy and I was very mechanical for my age, people always said so. But I didn't want to go gallivanting around the world. I spent a lot of time putting people in office; I thought I had an entrée for putting people in office to do good things, so that's what I did.

I decided to have my own shop, and that's exactly the way it came down. In the years I worked at the Wilsons', I was able to save up. My credit was pretty good at that time, so I just went ahead and bought the commercial machines I needed. I think I borrowed most of that money from the Third Northwestern Bank on Central Avenue in northeast Minneapolis, where the labor temple was. I think the bank was more predisposed to give me money because of all the labor people right there.

So in 1963, I opened my shop, Nellie's Alterations, on Nicollet Avenue. I was fifty-eight. When it was almost time for most people to think about retiring, I opened up a business. I really wanted the benefit of knowing and running the business, and to do the best in the time I had left to do it. I knew I would be pushed hard to put together a health and insurance policy for myself. What I really wanted I never got because I was too old to be completely covered. It turned out not to be easy, so I stayed with what my union had. I stayed on the executive board of my union, and kept the insurance by being a delegate to the Central Labor Body. Our insurance policy covered the executive board.

I opened my first store while I was still working at Wilsons'. It was in my house at 1302 Penn Avenue North, over a flower shop—actually in a room on the second floor. I remember way back when a Dr. Cohen lived there; his daughters had lived there until the apartment got too cramped. So I moved in, and what they used as a living room, I used as a shop. They tore that building down sometime in the '80s. It was known for a long time as Link's Flower Shop.

I bought myself every special machine I could. I bought a blind stitcher and a serger. At that time money was at a premium. Those machines were seven hundred to thirteen hundred dollars a machine. After I had bought a three-thread serger for seven hundred dollars, I needed a five-thread serger, which was thirteen hundred dollars. It did two operations—two spools did one and the other three did the other. The operation was shortening sleeves; that machine cost a lot but it made a lot. Most men are short-armed, you learn that in my business. I also learned a lot of men have big fat necks, too—too big and fat. Being married, you just generally know about a man's frailties, but these don't show up unless you buy a lot of shirts.

I was anxious enough to know what I wanted to go into, and I wasn't too afraid about investing in those machines. With all the work I was able to do, the five-thread serger paid for itself in a year.

But I wanted the same style shop the Wilsons had, a small shop, with small prices, but with business accumulating hand over fist. I had so much going for me—machinery, good relationships with wholesalers because they were then DFL. I'm a PR animal, too.

You don't need to be Superman or Superwoman, but it is all about hard work to get ahead. When I had my business, I structured it so my competition would be exactly what I wanted to be. I decided to do some of the hardest operations without too many others cluttering up the field. I did shirt alteration and zipper repair—you couldn't hardly find anyone to do that last one. A lot of my young relatives didn't want to get into my business, because they didn't want to work like hell. But I had a good business until the last day I worked, 1996, when I was ninety-one years old!

I had contracts with all the stores. I had Donaldson's, Rothschild's, Juster's and Ecklund's at University or Central Avenue. Dayton's? I wouldn't take Dayton's—they'd work me half to death. Wilsons' had Dayton's, and Dayton's didn't have one shirt shop, they had lots of shirt shops. I knew how they treated Wilsons'—like dirt. Worked them half to death, move up the time of the service they needed, then be slow to pay. I did all the Dayton's work for Wilsons', because I was fast and good. They came after me after I opened downtown, asking if I wanted to take their account, and I sort of put them off.

Then a funny thing happened: Douglas Dayton was on a community committee, something like the Urban Coalition today, where you get together with different factions of the community. Douglas came up to me and said, "I understand you have your own business, do you have the Dayton's account?" And I said no, but I didn't say I didn't want it. I grabbed my tongue back in my head—not that I did that very often! I made diplomatic talk since it was a nice, big account after all.

Then another funny thing happened. The big old boys from Dayton's corporate offices came over to my shop to have me do their work. Dayton's employees of various shirt departments would corner me to do work. They knew what the other shops did, but they knew what I could do. They were under pressure to provide good service, and they knew I could do good work quickly. So I sort of slid into doing Dayton's business, but on my own terms.

As the word about my work spread, sometimes people would have the nerve to say to me, "I didn't know someone as skilled as you came out of the black community." I said to them, "I could even build you a house!"—kind of flipping off to them.

Race did sometimes play a part. One time, a man came to my door, I just saw him. He had asked my neighbor about where the alteration shop was, and when my neighbor said right there, he looked in, and just turned right around. I think it was because I was black.

It was funny how things would come around from my first days of having to look so hard for a place to sew. I remember a man, in my First Avenue North store, who always brought his shirts to me. He was heavyset, almost Mr. Five-by-Five—that's what I used to call him. He was a member at the Athletic Club, ate too much food and drank too much whiskey. I always had to cut his sleeves down several inches.

He said to me one day, "Nellie, I'm glad you're around, there's hardly anybody in town to do this kind of work." He finally said he wouldn't take his shirts anywhere else. I don't know why it hit me then, but I had to remind him of some history—that he owned a business that wouldn't hire me when I was once looking for a job.

My niece, Pat Patterson, was working for me at the time, and when I told him this, her ears got as big as all outdoors! But I had told her that I was turned down back then because they all asked how would I know all that fine work?

When I reminded Mr. Five-by-Five of this, he got pretty upset. He said, "Well, you just lost a customer." And I just came right back at him; I told him, "You'll be back."

My niece Pat looked at me like I just lost my mind. Sure enough, two or three weeks later, he brought some shirts in. What did I do? I just gave him a long look.

I had to remind my niece that I was a public-relations animal. I told her I can sniff out situations and tell what's going to happen— almost beyond the call of humanity, almost like a hyena. You can almost believe it yourself if you're not sane. But one thing's for sure: I knew what the business world was, being out there in the field my whole life.

I usually had two employees, though I was the main production person right up until the end. One did sewing, and then I had one in as a preparer, a ripper. I didn't have a union contract because I was enough union in my shop as it was. I always paid union wages, vacation, eight-hour days, everything except having a health program.

I was too small to afford one. Most of them carried their own insurance from prior unions they had been in.

I wasn't being inconsistent here because we never tried to organize shops that small when I was organizing. How do you organize a two- or three-person shop under a union contract? A new business can't afford that, and yes, we in the union did take that as an excuse from a number of people who wanted to get that business off the ground. In a case like a sewing shop, it usually took at least ten or fifteen people.

I think I treated people pretty well, because mostly I had the same people. Neither one of them wanted that exact full-time job.

My shop was different from the Wilsons'—they ran a pretty sophisticated shop with four or five people. Their income and their floor of operation were different than mine. I didn't inherit any money, or get money from my parents like they did. But so far as training, I was much better, because my workers had the privilege of learning skills and becoming top-notch workers. I remember one woman, she was a saleswoman from Donaldson's to the private women's colleges. She was very intelligent, wanted to pay me to train her daughter rather than sending her to college. Other shops would keep people in the same tasks, but that limits training, and a person who lacks skills won't make as much money for employers. Very few owners say they can afford to train people, though that seems crazy to me. I was willing to take a chance on certain people if they were ever going to get the same skills I had.

The whole time I had my business, I never worked less than twelve hours a day, sometimes sixteen-hour days. I still have sewing dreams.

Chapter 20

National Democratic Politics

After I got out into my own business, I was working very hard, but I also was my own boss, so I had the flexibility to do more politics. I guess I was more effective with the time I had. I knew much more about business and education to put into the political arena. Like now, when someone raises a knotty issue, I can visualize the way it will go without much concentration, because of my experience.

I had been around long enough that a lot of people I worked with, or for, were becoming big national figures. Martin Luther King probably isn't the best example of someone I worked closely with. I was older than he was. We raised dollars for him starting in the '50s, but I only met him two or three times.

I was close enough to know this: Martin Luther King was trained by members of the labor movement—at first, he didn't know a damn thing about politics and education.

> The A. Philip Randolph people, you know, zeroed in around Martin Luther King. A fellow by the name of E. D. Nixon [from the Brotherhood of Sleeping Car Porters] was the person that plucked Martin Luther King. The rest of the ministers, [the labor people] didn't have much regard for them because they weren't too honest and all that, said, "This man hasn't a chance to get corrupted yet." E. D. Nixon said, "we'll pluck him, we'll anoint him" or whatever. (MHS, 45)

Sometimes, people don't realize how much the old-timers and the labor people did for civil rights.

During the big riots we had on Plymouth Avenue in [1968], I didn't know if I was going to get burned out or not because I lived right on Penn and Plymouth. Those fires came pretty close to me—came within a block. I was frustrated that that's the way the younger generation knew how to fight back. I wasn't mad at them, I was frustrated. I wanted them to learn the philosophical things about fight back.

I believe a hundred percent in the right to strike, and that can be one of the most violent and bomb-throwing things. Not that working people have the right to start it.

I suppose someplace along the line, these people believed there had to be a little violence. But I'm very strong in the educational field, and so were my parents, and I guess I had the advantage of people who were realistic, down-to-earth, believers in the things of life, about how to really change things.

I thought burning and bomb throwing was wrong because you're likely to burn up some people. You can't be a supporter of humane issues and put people in danger like that.

But Martin Luther King was an amazing man who learned well. His political consciousness grew so much that by the time of his death I could find no fault with him. Let me tell you something that happened. When he came to Chicago prior to his death, there were such a large number of black people employed by the sanitation department of Chicago that he came in trying to help. One of the labor papers there asked me what I thought of him and how it was going. I said, if he keeps talking the way he is, about labor, that blacks need to join unions, someone's going to take a potshot at him. I mean, there were labor people in Minnesota who had been jailed for organizing at one time, just for organizing.

I was flashing back to this one man from the Teamsters I knew quite well, named William Sennett, and I got him on the board of the local NAACP. He was a business agent for the Teamsters, put in jail in the 1930s in North Dakota for many years to rot. All you had to do to be jailed in some places then was talk for union organizing. This was before Franklin Roosevelt put forth laws that gave union organizers some protection. Year after year, at the Central Labor Body, we put nickels and dimes together to get him out. When he finally did, I figured with his tenacity, as someone who fought for people to have a roof over their head and be able to eat, he was the right person for the board of the NAACP, so I nominated him. The boards could fill their own vacant spots, so I just lobbied the board to bring him on.

Anyway, just days later, Martin Luther King went to Tennessee and got shot. I guess that was the potshot I was talking about. I sat with King's father, right next to him at the 1976 Democratic convention. Jimmy Carter kept an eye on Reverend King the whole time. King's father, he wasn't for Carter originally, but by then he was. When Carter accepted Mondale as his vice president, that did it for the elder Mr. King.

I found Jimmy Carter a decent man, a moral person, also one of the most intellectual presidents we ever had. I thought his intelligence brought him around to the basics, that equality is the right thing to do. He talked about it so much in the South, I'm surprised he's still living.

Around the time that Carter and Mondale were elected to the White House, I made a serious run for the Democratic National Committee from Minnesota. The DNC is the power of the Democratic Party through the whole United States. They bring together what the rank-and-file Democrats want as far as the national platform, and all of the committees, within the framework of the national Democrat Party. They are the apparatus that brings the groups together.

I mean, when you've been in the party as long as I have, you'd like to help run things at the national level. I had thought about going for the DNC before, but every time I thought of it, about ten women had gotten to campaign before me. Finally, about 1976, I was runner-up for the DNC position, which was done by a vote of the state DFL central committee.

The way I got on was this: a woman named Ruth Cain was the assistant chair for the DFL in Minnesota; she was an automatic member of the Democratic National Committee. By this time, 1978, Rudy

Perpich was governor. About 1978, he put her on the Railroad and Warehouse Commission, a regular commission on freight and taxation. When he did that, she had to step down from the DNC, and that put me on it.

I served from 1979 to 1988, and I enjoyed every minute of it. There was a big social side, and from time to time I got to go to Washington on party business. Because of that I've been to Teddy Kennedy's house across the river in Maryland many times. I remember he always had lots of cheese, crackers, always plenty to drink—I mean, alcoholic beverages. It was like going into an art gallery. The basement was right on a river bank, with a walk on three sides, wide-open windows, artwork, pictures of the Kennedys. I enjoyed that if nothing else.

I had the privilege of meeting Jackie Onassis and her sister, Princess Radziwill. I had met Jackie's late husband—the president, I mean—a couple of times when he visited here. I liked what he stood for, but I couldn't stand his baby brother Bobby because he went after Jimmy Hoffa in the 1950s. I could see the demise of labor in that. They wanted to kill off what Hoffa stood for. Hoffa was a good human person. He might have been tied up on the periphery with mobsters, but he was so dedicated. I could see through what his mob stuff was—kind of like the old saying, you join 'em to get rid of 'em. I think that's where Jimmy was coming from—he believed in his membership all the way. You know the Teamsters under his regime had the best health program in the United States. Of any organization! There were a lot of people in Detroit who would not own property if not for what he did, putting them into leadership. A lot of them were on the coalition of black trade unions, and there are still some old, old-timers around. For most of the poor families in Detroit, Hoffa loaned them money. People of color thought he was quite a person and supported him. It comes right back to what I just said, his real concern was about rank-and-file membership.

Three thousand dollars is what Bobby Kennedy had against Hoffa—that's what got it started, when Kennedy accused Hoffa of stealing three thousand dollars from, the people against him said, the health fund. But I never believed it and they never proved it.

I just barely met Hoffa once at a convention, which is just about like not knowing. But I know the writings on him better than just about anybody else, better than the Teamsters.

Dave Beck, a racketeer out of Washington, was president of the Teamsters and spent the rank and file's money like water. As far as I knew, he was doing things before he became the Teamsters' president. He had a house in Seattle and built a swimming pool so he could entertain the bosses with poolside parties. But Jimmy Hoffa, he was a very down-to-earth person who took care of the rank and file.

I think some of the more recent stories about Hoffa being in a cement block someplace, I think that could be very real. Some of the mobsters probably killed him. The Teamsters were such a lucrative organization, in terms of money and power.

The mob really wanted to muscle in on the Hotel and Restaurant Workers when I was there; they tried hard in our Chicago and Evanston chapters. But if you do your education job, before a lot of stuff happens, you tell key members that the enemy is there. There's a way you do those things, if you're just a little bit smart. You just don't bleat it everywhere you go.

I saw them try to win an election in Milwaukee in 1947, just try to take a spot on the International Hotel and Restaurant Workers board. We just outvoted them.

And I ask you, what's the difference between the FBI and the mobsters? We had a couple of people from the FBI on our executive board of Local 665 in the beginning.

Bobby Kennedy went after Hoffa, I think, to gain a little power. The corporate world still wanted to kill off labor, kill off a lot of what Roosevelt had done. It wasn't a JFK philosophy—it was like a lot of families, they had differences. Bobby Kennedy was always able to capture the press at the right time. He did a much better job than his brother did with associating with the issues.

It seemed to me Bobby was a political tyrant, the way he campaigned for his brother in 1960. Between Minnesota's and Iowa's caucuses, the campaign rented cars from here to Des Moines. He didn't give any quarter to the people working for his brother—if they were sick, how old they were. I really didn't like that.

I think to some extent Bobby Kennedy got enlightened toward his death. Gene McCarthy did make mention of Bobby Kennedy becoming very good on minority issues. He said he wets his finger and holds it to the wind on a lot of other matters.

Me and Mary Ryan put on the first coffee party for Gene when he was running for president in 1968. She was on the board of the Unity House in north Minneapolis. That was a community house, like the Phyllis Wheatley House, that rampaged during the depression and on through the 1950s, a largely church-based thing that took care of the poor and community folk, and provided what we call today social services.

I couldn't support Hubert because of the Vietnam War issue, which he supported at the time. Early on, as Johnson's vice president, a lot of Hubert's speeches and positions were written by Texas Democrats. John Connally and other conservatives who ran to the Republicans. They were still part of the Democratic coalition at the time.

I was against Vietnam because, like in World War Two, I had read about the percentages of blacks being killed in the war. It had gotten to the point that forty-two percent of the field troops killed were black. That tightened me up, stiffened me up. Why couldn't Hubert see that?

The war was another one that Hubert and I didn't discuss. I wished I had. Cecil Newman had talked to him for the black press, he may have printed editorials about it. It wasn't a question of not getting to Hubert, I did see him at a couple of coffee parties. There were other things, at other people's houses, but you just don't bring up those things there. I understand a lot of the opposition to Hubert, but a lot of that opposition frightened me.

Sometimes you have to be very strategic and politic about your principles and supporting a candidate. You don't have to compromise on a position, but you can maintain it without taking a hard position for or against somebody.

There were a couple of people in Humphrey's campaign that wished I was over there, but when I laid out the reasons for supporting Gene, they didn't have much to say.

Hubert was so far ahead of most people in the area of the rights of people—but he knew Gene had a hell of a record in that field, too. I was one of the first ones to call Gene McCarthy "Clean Gene," because politically he was always very clean. In the fifties, whenever we needed support in the Fourth Congressional District, St. Paul, Gene came through for us. I had more trouble in my own district, because Clark McGregor, a Republican, represented it for a while. I still don't know how he got in.

When Gene McCarthy was in Congress, he had a perfect record on civil and human rights. Both he and his wife, Abigail, came out of the Federation of Teachers, which is what made them both pretty good labor people.

When I went for Gene for senator in the '50s, I got in a lot of trouble with my lady friends. They wanted Eugenia Anderson, who of course would have been the first woman senator from here, but I stuck with Gene. Eugenia was a good friend of Hubert's. I wasn't for her because I was one of the founders of the Fair Employment Practices Commission for the city of Minneapolis. Hubert went to bat for her as chair of the commission, but she could never see any problems on a report with something about people of color. She was wealthy, very much of a lady, and I don't know if she knew how bad the situation was for working people. Bill Craddock of the local NAACP was vice-chair; anytime a complaint would come up, Eugenia would pigeonhole it and Bill would come right out of the meeting and tell me. I am a hundred percent hard-nosed into the job situation, so no way could I support Eugenia. I wouldn't try to get her unappointed—that would be stepping on the toes of friends, not just political associates. I didn't want to clobber Hubert either. I did let her know how I felt.

In the end, I voted for Hubert in 1968, but doing it the way I did it, I didn't lose any face on policy or basic principle I believed in. Overall, I was a heck of a lot more loyal to the party than some of the DNC people were. In 1968, our two DNC people were not covering the DNC office too well for Humphrey when he was candidate for president. Actually, what happened is that the Texas Democrats were running the DNC, from LBJ having been in power, but as long as they had two outstanding people from Minnesota and a presidential candidate from Minnesota, well, for some reason they just didn't have good national fund-raising lists!

Chapter 21

Campaign Manager

1979: The Campaign

Nellie worries about the North Side
and about who speaks for her people
in the councils of power. When she leaves
the shop at night, she watches the faces
of the kids on the corner of Plymouth and Penn,
sees the desperation in their eyes, feels them
letting go of life, ready to kill or be killed, no matter.

She knows they have no jobs, that the joy
of work has been denied to them. She knows nearly half
of them will be in prison before they are thirty.
For years she has headed the jobs program
at the Urban League, finding union work for a thousand
black and brown men and women. The LEAP program
is the bedrock of her beliefs: civil rights and labor together,
creating jobs and access to education,
to housing, to hope and to dignity.

But now the hilt has grown steep, and she needs help,
looks for a new voice inside the circle to tell the truth
about these streets and the despair that lives there.
She picks Van White to run for City Council,
a decent man, a hard worker and a man

with a record of working for others in the community.
No black man or woman has ever served on the Council,
but Nellie knows he can be elected. She begins
to call in markers earned with sweat over fifty years.

White is a good candidate, clear and strong
in his views. Nellie goes door to door for him,
passes out leaflets at churches and clubs,
and brings in Labor to do voter registration.
Her long stride is a little stiffer; her eyes
can no longer pick out familiar faces in the crowd.
On the block, everyone is so young, and must
be educated again, she says, from the beginning.

The pundits at the *Star and Tribune* smile among
themselves at Nellie, in the streets again.
"Of course, everyone loves Nellie," they say,
"but her time has passed. She doesn't understand
the Black community today, doesn't understand '80s politics,
a relic from another age. Time to hang it up."
But at the polls in September, White is nominated
and later wins the seat on Council, where he will
serve for ten years. On the North Side,
there is some hope again, and new leadership.

In her small apartment in senior citizens housing
on Hennepin, Nellie is asleep in front of the television.
Piles of paper—newspapers and pamphlets,
posters and campaign pictures—lie all about her.
She dreams of a clearing in the deep pine woods
north of Hinckley, of a family reunion, a field
filled with laughing children and long picnic tables
piled with chicken and corn-on-the-cob
and apple pie and coffee. Herbert Harvey
is a boy again, sitting on his aunt's knee.

They are a free people, the Allens,
a family at home on their land,
in Minnesota, in America,
And free.

From "Nellie at Ninety"
(Robert L. Carothers, 1995)

Just think: some sixty-four percent of our black youth are jobless today, and my blood boils when I think of the man some of our community leaders wanted to support. He wanted to phase out the only skills training program introduced by the Urban League through the LEAP program. (Nellie Stone Johnson, letter to the editor, *Twin Cities Courier,* February 23, 1978)

————

Although World War II was just winding down when Nellie became Minneapolis's first black elected official, by 1979, the voters had still not elected a person of color to the City Council.

————

In '74, '75, whatever, I was still pounding the pavement, doing grassroots organizing for various causes. Which ones? I was almost seventy, but I knew my part of town. I'd been planning on running someone for the City Council for a long time. Like anything, at first it was just a thought. I was thinking who could run, and the only person who had experience besides myself was Van White.

I don't remember who exactly I was mad about in that letter to the editor, but the big thing for me with Van White was that he had a fairly good reputation in areas I liked—housing and the jobs situation, and government support for that. He was usually the first black person involved in those programs, such as the Pilot City project in north Minneapolis and the Willard-Homewood neighborhood housing committee.

I had met him when he was in the Department of Economic Security, which was the old Department of Jobs and Training. I went on its board in 1972.

Van was a tough hombre. He came out of a working-class family, was raised by his grandma. He didn't know anything about hard-nosed politics, but God—I cut my teeth on it!

I was seventy-four when I ran Van's race, but it went well. I knew what I was doing. I told Van, if you really let me manage your campaign I will make you council member of Minneapolis. Other people may tell you what's good for your campaign, but don't bother me with it. I've heard it all.

I ran the campaign by doing the old-fashioned politics that I knew how to do under the auspices of every candidate of the Farmer-Labor Party. Even though we call ourselves DFLers now, it was the Farmer-Laborers that really got out there and worked for its candidates, at the grassroots level, door knocking and meetings. There wasn't a whole lot of TV or anything you needed big money for in a City Council race, so the hard workers still had a tremendous advantage.

You have to get out there and touch your political base, person-to-person, go to meetings at houses, go to every political thing. I did all of those things; whenever anyone contacted us, we were there. I was pretty tight with campaign funds—we ran it for about five thousand dollars. One big expense is that every time there was a group fundraiser or coffee in the district, I always bought a ticket for Van.

There was an old adage that came up in Van's campaign: in the black community, people wait for the general election to vote. But I went from one end of the ward to the other telling them that the primary was the election. A Republican wasn't going to win there.

When I was managing Van's campaign, a lot of people said, "Nellie, it should be you that's running." What I'm saying is that no one gave me a chance of winning that seat with me running Van *and* bucking the local DFL machine.

At that time, the *Star Tribune* called them the North Side Machine, or the North Side Mafia. The way I took it, they just did not want to let me or anyone serious in the community of color have any political influence. Some of the northsiders were good at times—state representative Jim Rice, you couldn't beat him on jobs, but we fought like cats and dogs over different people we liked for elective positions.

Van's opponent was a woman named Dorothy James; all of the regular Democrats supported her. The City Council president at the time, Lou DeMars, campaigned hard for Dorothy to be elected. There was little there beyond using her to a hilt—if she had to put her head in a burning stove, she'd do it. Van was a little more independent than that. Lou and I were friends from the North Side—I secondarily came by him because I was good friends of his father, Cyril DeMars, who was a good labor person. But Lou and I didn't always fit in the same part of the power structure, and we weren't always on the same side, especially on local issues.

But, see, I was the only person who was black who had won citywide other than school board. The DFL leadership was saying my candidate couldn't win, but they should have known better than that! I said, thank you very much, I know what I am doing, and I can count votes very well. I always knew I could win. Hard numbers count, not some expert opinion of what people are going to do. I've always believed that, and I'm still that way.

We had people coming out of the woodwork to help the campaign. The thing was, I had such a reputation of beating people up on racism that they wouldn't even get on that track of being racist towards Van. It wasn't that everybody felt it was time to elect a black council candidate, but that he was strong on jobs and training across the board. I made Van into what he was—a guy strong on those issues across the board. That was our message, and we just hammered it.

When Van won, we had a party at the old Produce Bank Building. Ol' Lou didn't even stop to shake hands with me. He just gave me a big old hug and said, you scoundrel, you pulled it off! He was very smart about recognizing the winner. He knew he'd have to start working with Van, and that we were all DFLers anyway.

Afterward Van asked me to be his chief aide. That usually happens with campaign managers. I think I could've had a record that was second to none, but once again, I wasn't looking for a job out of this. Part of it was about helping labor—I put fifty percent of the labor people together with him. In the black community, labor was very important, even more so in 1979 than today. The big prize was not just getting a black man elected, but a strong friend of labor. A lot of people never got past Van's race, but when you've been fighting for the right things across the board as long as I have, you see the big picture.

Chapter 22

Rudy

Rudy Perpich was Minnesota's longest-serving governor. Although a dentist by training, the Croatian-born Perpich epitomized the immigrant- and labor-dominated Iron Range in northeastern Minnesota, the most loyal DFL territory in the state.

I don't want to make any bones about this: Rudy Perpich was my favorite governor.

It wasn't like I had known him forever. I had met Rudy Perpich and his brothers prior to him becoming lieutenant governor in 1972, when he was a legislator, but I didn't really know him. I met him sometime in the sixties. I don't remember around what issue at all. It was difficult with the fly-by-night meetings you get into in the legislature, to psych out his philosophy. I'm sure at some point he was psyching me out, too.

I supported him for lieutenant governor when he was running with Wendy Anderson in 1972. I was supporting Rudy—I didn't have to sit down with him. His record was strong from the Eighth [Congressional] District. He and George and Tony, his brothers, their labor record was known, and it was enough. His record was one hundred percent.

I was very active in the party then, and I was working hard to get Rudy votes at the convention in 1972. There was a big problem with that because Elmer Childress, a black man from the Communications

Workers, was running for secretary of state, and you had to appeal to people to vote for both of them.

The problem was, Elmer was not kind of sharp on the politics, and he ruled me out of his political operation. He had Tom Tipton as his chair, and Tom couldn't find his way across the street. I think Tom may have been a Republican then, but he was riding my back at the convention trying to meet labor people. Elmer had thirty-five to forty years in the labor movement, and he had a record of doing the right things for people of color. I think the weak link was his lack of sophistication and guts in not being a part of the Equal Opportunity program. His philosophy was to deal with people one-on-one, but his weakness was not taking a political position and standing up for it. I'd been part of every program like that since we had gotten the Fair Employment Practices Act in Minneapolis in 1947 and never stopped.

The only person who was hard-hitting about that at that convention was me! People have to be geared sometimes towards things human. Basically, we had instituted in the platform, equal opportunity in every form.

Elmer was not hitting the equal opportunity thing hard enough. We were not getting our fair share of what the Constitution provided for—equal opportunity for all. The other side of it was that Elmer was not hitting the labor base hard enough—no way Tom Tipton, strictly a white-collar person, could do that. We managed to find enough votes to get Elmer and Rudy nominated, but Elmer lost in the primary.

I had now done some heavy lifting for Rudy, and Rudy never forgot that. Rudy and I got closer and closer after he got in as lieutenant governor. Rudy had a very hearty laugh—you could hear it for miles around, but when he got mad, it was like the proverbial bull spitting fire. They say that about Clinton, but that doesn't always come through. Rudy couldn't hide anything. But Rudy and I were a natural—we never argued about anything!

He had big dreams and somehow he made even the wildest things happen. He made some comments to me that he wanted to build a Minnesota college in Japan. I said, Rudy, with you we're likely to build a college in Timbuktu! I was for it, I guess, but when we went to Japan, I knew he was right. People were self-reliant—everybody worked, everybody studied. I liked the kids having uniforms. It kept down the competition that takes the mind off of studies.

He was a strong supporter of school programs; he talked about it, came to a lot of meetings. I was trying to get my scholarship program going, to help minority people get educated in the state college system. We had a fund-raiser; he and Lola, his wife, both came. I've got three honorary certificates from governors for my education work.

We did trust each other—we absolutely trusted each other. It was very simple and to the point. That trust was laced up with a philosophical understanding and belief that went into a great deal of legislation. We believed in the Constitution and that all people should be treated equal in their rights as human beings.

One of the most important ones: we believed that people would succeed if they had a job and were not discriminated against because of color. It's kind of like women with sexual harassment, though I've always said that as a woman, racial harassment is ten times as worse. Sexual harassment, that's usually one person, but with racism, a family of ten people can be hurt by job discrimination.

People like Rudy Perpich firmly believed in people working. I don't know if anyone believed in it more firmly, except me. To him, that was the cure for almost everything.

> People feel good about themselves when they're working. All these other things people come up with, housing programs and youth programs and all that, that's all well and good. But somewhere in each family there has to be a job. And that job begets housing and also makes it possible for people to get the education they want. It creates the *desire* for education. Out of that comes everything else. (CP)

Through Rudy, I could get what I wanted. He would always be receptive to my argument: if there are weak pockets in the system, address them specifically. If there's a shortage of jobs, get more jobs. If there's a shortage of training, get more of that.

That's one reason the LEAP program came about. We negotiated one of the best programs in the world, in the construction trades, for people of color—the Labor Education Advancement Program. It provided job training for young minorities, the apprenticeships they were not getting. We needed a state program that would fund education and training for minorities, especially because the federal government was cutting back.

There had been a national-type program that had been supported by the national Urban League, which got money from corporations and the national Labor Department—and I wanted to get away from both. I didn't want to deal with Southern Democrats or those elite people on boards.

Those Democrats and Republicans eventually cut off funding from the Labor Department, and sure enough, the national Urban League board didn't put up much of a fight, because they were too close to the corporations they needed support from.

When Vernon Jordan became executive secretary of the Urban League, he didn't understand what we were talking about when we fought reverse discrimination. Here's what I always said: if I owned Dayton-Hudson, or media outfits like KSTP and WCCO, and I only hired blacks, *then* we could talk about reverse discrimination. Then Vernon Jordan and I had an argument because he was out there fronting for the corporate world.

It was at a reception that we, the board of the Urban League, had at the IDS Center, right in the throes of being thrown out of an organization as an affiliate. We argued about just how much each part of the Urban League was really doing for education and training. [Jordan] got off our back as an Urban League affiliate, but he tried to hurt our reputation even as he wrote letters praising the glorious work we were doing on discrimination.

I also was dealing with people like Ron Brown, who was then in charge of national legislation for the national Urban League. He just didn't have the enthusiasm and knowledge and political beliefs to understand how important a program like this was. He just really kind of turned me off—like with Vernon Jordan; you could see he didn't want to upset the corporations too much.

The Ron Browns of the world just didn't show enough enthusiasm for the total program. It made me wish Hubert Humphrey were still living; Ron Brown would have paid a lot of attention to federal labor programs.

Hubert had died in 1978, but at least we were able to talk of a few issues before he died. We never avoided each other after 1968—it could have happened on his part, but I never noticed that. It never happens to me, because I'm such a down-to-earth person. I'll just sit down and talk with anyone.

These were mostly at political meetings, where you have that offshoot of talk and communication, sitting and talking over a cup of coffee. Near the end, we talked about basically where we were going as a DFL party. We talked about the good old days of when we were organizing, getting back to some of those basic principles, grassroots work. I guess both of us were saying that the party needed to do more of that.

When Hubert died, I felt so bad, of course—I felt like a member of his family. I wasn't at the funeral, I was sick in bed, but I was all ready to go. I went to the wake a couple of times, stood on the capitol steps and nearly froze. I didn't make a speech, but I talked one-on-one. Every time I turned around, there was another old-time DFLer. Hubert's legacy is people, just simply that. The things he did for the ordinary people in the state of Minnesota.

Now there are only two of the forty-two LEAP programs left—Omaha and here. There just wasn't the pressure to fund them adequately, not enough organization and advocacy for the empowerment of young black workers. That's why I wanted to bring a state program to Minnesota in the first place.

The national office of the Urban League cut us off in '84, cut us off completely. When they did, [local Urban League head] Gleason Glover felt very bad, because he was one of these elite guys. He went to the McKnight Foundation, got some money to run it for six months to a year. I looked at the situation. The best program in the country, we can't have this going hand-to-mouth. So I starting laying the groundwork with the governor.

Me and Rudy decided at breakfast to do it in Minnesota, at the governor's mansion. Maybe I shouldn't call it that. Rudy hated the mansion—he called it "the house." He hated anyone who called it the mansion. That was just one sign of how populist he felt.

I remember calling Rudy's security people to say I wanted to have coffee with Rudy, that we had something important to talk about, and then I started to say my name was Nellie and the man I was talking to stopped me. "Oh, Nellie, we know who you are," the person said.

When Rudy and I talked, he said, "Well, where do we go for money?" I had my eye on the Department of Labor and Industry. During the session, the feminists came on me because I was that close to Rudy and knew where the money was.

It was funny, because I had been so close to Hubert Humphrey on many issues, just like I became with Rudy. There were people who said, for God's sake, don't let her get close to Rudy Perpich, too! But too bad—I was. After Perpich, someone I knew heard them say, "We'll never give her another governor she can have in her hip pocket."

Many feminists want to kill off the black worker training programs—and that includes the ones for black women! When I was chair of the Urban League training programs, I was trying to get votes for training at the legislature, and I needed St. Paul votes, from their delegation. I sat down and there were a couple of empty chairs next to me. One gal sat down and I said to myself, I wonder what damn thing she wanted. She was talking to me, she got so carried away with herself—like the meeting was in Albania or some damn place. She asked me where the training dollars would come from and I said, that's for me to know and you to find out! She wanted that money for her own causes, and she was doing research against me.

I negotiated with Minneapolis and St. Paul legislators to get LEAP through. Unfortunately, Randy Staten [then a north Minneapolis representative] didn't know what to do and sent it to the wrong committee, which was pretty hostile to it, for money or reverse-discrimination reasons, I don't remember which. He needed to get unanimous consent to pull it out of there, and that was tough because you needed all the Republicans to go along, too. So I was trying to get a hundred percent of the votes for it, and Fred Norton [DFL House Speaker] said he'd do it. He was there for it, and he made sure he got the votes to get it out of even that committee. Jim Rice, from north Minneapolis, was a power for labor in the legislature, and we started knocking down people together. There was no splitting us up, we were a powerful group.

The sad part is that the state's commitment to apprentice training has really faded since Rudy was governor. I'm close to the white building trades people, who have the best human philosophy—we held hands and believed in solidarity. Don Early, and Ray Waldron, president of the state building trades. Tom Hansen of the plumbers—he was a research person I practically raised. I didn't get as much support from the Urban League. And of course the antilabor feeling cuts across the whole country.

I think even white-collar unions like AFSCME [the American Federation of State, County, and Municipal Employees] don't help, either. That's the reason AFSCME is as flaky as it is: they're white collar, not really dealing with the hard issues of equality for all races in health care, equal opportunity, education. They got theirs and it seems like those that are shut out they don't really want in. You'd like to see them put the two together—on a good general education emphasis with training, such as LEAP—and go all the way for it. MAPE [the Minnesota Association of Professional Employees, another public-sector union] is the same way.

Rudy gave me money for any liberal thing I wanted. I was responsible for five sitting judges; I don't brag about that too much—there are too many peons who get jealous of me. We proposed them out of our whole organization, the local Urban League, when I was on the board. When it came to judges, Rudy listened to his friends quite a bit.

One of our biggest wins was when Rudy helped get the Mall of America built in the late 1980s. I remember flying on a Northwest

Airline plane to Edmonton with Rudy to meet the Ghermezian brothers [the original promoters of the megamall], who lived there. There was silver service, china. I never dreamed Northwest Airlines would own china! They wanted me to be there to represent the African American community, and I wanted to be there to talk about affirmative action in the megamall construction. The local Urban League and the NAACP, they were messing up and trying to tone down the language. One young man there, from the black community, Jesse Overton, he worked for Honeywell-Bull Corporation. His role was to work with me to get an affirmative action plan for the megamall. Don Early also carried the ball for that. Some of those people in the black community were green-eyed with envy about me being one of the people on the trip, but together, those of us who were there made sure affirmative action was respected.

— Chapter 23 —

Out to Africa

It was kind of a strange way my trip to Africa all came about. I was in Duluth, at a Coalition of Trade Union Women meeting. This was July 1980. I was going up the steps when I came back home and I heard my phone—it was Dick Moe, Walter Mondale's aide, from Washington. Mondale was vice president of the United States by this time. Dick Moe said, "Where the hell have you been?" He said to get myself to Africa!

I put up all the excuses—I've got business in Minnesota. Moe was trying to do my business, but I knew my business better than he did. I didn't have a plane ticket—I didn't even have a passport! He said, "Get your birth certificate," but I didn't have it on me. So he sent Pearl, from his office, to Hastings [the Dakota County seat] to get it! And I found out, when I looked at my birth certificate, they had me down as a boy! They had my mother's name wrong. The only thing right was my birth date and my father's name and the doctor's name and the office. It was enough for the passport office to deliver a new passport in two or three days. I found out how you can cut corners in Washington.

It was a trip for the State Department, diplomatic. I remember saying to someone, probably Dick Moe, me of all people! For the State Department! You know what they must have on me! They sent me to the FBI to get checked out for the trip. I remember this big burly man said, "Don't worry about a thing." I thought, I should be vice president of the United States!

I was not privileged to do too much official business on the trip. I remember saying to Fritz, "What I am here for?" He said, "We're going to see the green revolution, to see how people work and how they take care of their health." Put that way, with those issues, it felt just like home: the basic issues.

He also told people on the way out there, "Take good care of Nellie. She's old, but she's a tough old bird."

Our trip over there went something like this: out of Washington, we first landed in the Azores, where the U.S. had a big landing strip. Our first official stop was Dakar, Senegal, where things got off to a bang right away.

I played first lady the first night there. We were at a world-renowned restaurant—a restaurant on a pier. He and I went through all the motions of being top dog.

Walter's wife, Joan, passed me on the way in and said it was O.K. to walk in on his arm. I thought to myself, by the grace of God, I turned out right! He escorted me to a spot at the head of a large table, and I broke out in gooseflesh! I hadn't known the protocol. I mean, I wasn't exactly used to these official-type dinners. I only had one dress, a long skirt that I could put on and look protocolish, if you will.

Me and Fritz just carried on! Joan was on the other side of the table. She gave me a wave that said, "How are you doing?"

I got to know croissants well with Mondale, in Senegal. We ate a lot of them in the hotel because they came from France and England, and we were told only to eat stuff from Europe. The other thing we could drink was beer, and I bought myself a bottle of cognac. I figured there was nothing in the world that alcohol wouldn't kill before I went to bed.

It wasn't all caviar and champagne while we were over there, I don't want to give you that idea. When we were still in Senegal, I visited the Island of Goré—that was a big place for them to ship the slaves from. There were chains and long pens to hold people. When I was learning geography, we did learn about that place, and I always pronounced it *gore,* like being gored by a bull. It's really *gor-ay,* but after I saw it, I said my pronunciation was closer to being right than theirs.

Although I like to remind white people that I have people of many races in my family history, I do feel that Africa is my homeland, and when I do identify myself, it's always as black.

From Senegal, we went to our next official visit in Niamey, Niger. I remember a big mosque in Niamey—the whole northern part is Muslim. We visited a local school, and it was such crude, down-to-earth stuff, nothing modern. There was even a horse show I attended—there were a whole lot of old nags. Even in Niamey, I knew a horse from a nag.

In Nigeria, it felt the most like home—well, at least they spoke English. In the ten days we were gone, we spent the most time there. It was pretty good—it did not feel too safe, like a few areas of the American inner city.

When we were in Lagos, Nigeria's capital, we saw somewhat newer stuff—schools, health systems. But it was still fairly crude and not modern. I couldn't understand that in Nigeria. They were making money hand over fist from oil, but they had open sewers. All the people there couldn't just demand their share of the money. The military made sure of that.

Every country—Senegal, Niger, Nigeria—wanted money and help with crops and education, just about everything we live by here, only they had so much less. They didn't seek my advice—they were all talking at once with Fritz.

We did talk amongst ourselves every day. We'd meet, the whole group of us, in Congressman Charley Rangel's room. Fritz was the powerful man there, so he would command the bed. Another woman who was there was Penny Miller; she later died in a fire in St. Paul, but for many consecutive years, when I was chair of the Rules at the DFL convention, I wanted Penny to be secretary because she was so honest and fair. We became close friends. Benjamin Hooks, the president of the NAACP, was there, and Congressman Stokes and Al Eisele, a journalist, were there. Fritz and he had a mutual admiration society.

We talked about what we'd seen, about the social things, on how people actually lived. I leaned a lot on my own agenda to analyze it, but we all agreed about education leading to a better life there. The problem was just so big.

— Chapter 24 —

Fighting with the Feminists

More middle-class feminists should be helping minority
women. Some of them think they're God's gift to the political world. . . . Many are used as window dressing. . . . You can't
promote one group of women at the expense of others.

(MWP)

As far as I was concerned, I did more for women than most women in
the women's movement. I'm tough on the feminists because I'm a
third-, fourth-, fifth-generation feminist, and when I see one feminist
coming out for any kind of inequality, it makes me mad. I'm tougher
on them because they should be my allies. I can smell the women who
are out for themselves, and not for others—I can smell that a hundred
feet away.

A lot of people don't understand where we came from. I worked at
the Athletic Club, the den of animalism, where women just didn't
count. Those things shaped your beliefs, where you came from.
Remember, I was one of the first women on a union negotiating committee to get equal pay for women in the forties. But I had to fight
them to get it for black men, too, and that problem played out again
and again and again. When I look at the majority of women today
who take after the black male with their animalistic attacks, well, this
was happening then with no love lost. The feminists would placate

197

me in those days if they were doing labor stuff, because of my friendship with Hubert.

Equal pay was probably one of my main union accomplishments. The most discriminatory practices came down on my head from white women in labor and politics; they were too dumb to figure out where this equal opportunity came from. We said there has to be equal pay for women, regardless of ethnicity.

There was nothing funny about it to me. I am for jobs for women and minorities, but not to the extent that plays feminism off of black people. The lowest economically are black males, and the union pay is really good. They didn't start anyone else off at seventeen dollars an hour. We could have worked together, but when somebody thinks their power, because of their skin color, is above my knowledge or power, there's going to be a conflict.

For example, women in the trades. When I chaired the Labor Education program for the Urban League, I had a verbal fight with the feminists. The fights were about the ABCs of the politics. I wasn't about to say what I was doing. Who were my supporters, how to get the support of the legislature? They wanted to use the process of what we were doing to get our money. It got to be a little bit of a hassle for me. As a result, I later was no longer eligible or privileged to stay on the Democratic National Committee. Too often, it was minorities versus women.

The feminists would push quotas for women, but not for minorities, no sir. I thought that was hypocritical and wrong.

This all came up in the seventies when I said I opposed the Equal Rights Amendment, until they included women of color, to spell it out and say this includes women of color. I was on the Democratic National Committee, so I just attempted to get through the resolution demanding that at the state and national level. I was part of the DNC's black caucus, part of the labor caucus. No one could get anything passed by the DNC without getting it by us. We were a big part of the power structure.

I've been through too much civil and human rights work to know you have to spell that out in the Constitution. If things aren't spelled out, they can interpret things against you. People would say, "We've got all that in the Constitution." I would say that's not enough—we've got to spell out what those laws mean.

> In the 1950s, prior to *Brown v. Board of Education,* educators from all walks said, "You're in the Constitution" to justify the fairness of separate-but-equal. We'd have been right up against the same thing one more time. (CP)

I did proposed a couple of resolutions for this when I was on the DNC; people sounded like airheads, despite coming from high places, about the inclusion of women, but for the high echelon of the white middle class, not for anybody with a brown skin. They said we just can't support this because it was a quota. Women in the Democratic Party want a fifty percent equation on all committees, in education, but not for women of color. Some quit arguing with me on that.

I didn't give a damn what they said, I wanted the percentage of representation on committees and boards, state and national, that did include women of color. If they were fighting that hard to get their interests in the Constitution, well, I was going to get me in there, too. I think the white women there across the board—you can't lay this all on the white Southerners—felt they could lord their whiteness over everyone.

I've always been a feminist, just not one against the black male. The racism comes by overall actions. I say, don't use me, but they stay self-centered. The best recent example was Anita Hill. They wanted to go after Clarence Thomas when he was up for the Supreme Court, so they just brought some people of color out. I liked the way we went after Robert Bork better. You attack what his rulings are, what he's done, not what he is. The feminists used Anita Hill to the hilt, to get rid of Clarence Thomas, but they are not as smart as they think they are. She provided a good visual picture, but not the substance you needed to truly keep him from the Court.

The feelings and opposition of the black community didn't mean a damn thing to the feminists—but blacks didn't want Clarence Thomas, either. The thing is, no black person will let you do that to a guy, even if he is a bastard—just like the Jewish community won't let someone beat the hell out of people just because they are Jewish. Even if you don't like that person, you'll rally around him. And the way the feminists played it, that's exactly why Clarence Thomas is on the Court today.

I've never seen a group of people commit hara-kiri like women are now, losing everything they've got. They are losing power to go beyond even just salaries alone, into health programs. Their failure is to make common cause with people of color. They should just go out there on the old language of equal opportunity. Old language was equal opportunity to begin with, and then that phrase, regardless of race, creed, color, national origination, religious doctrine.

The heads of the black, Hispanic, and Native American committees, it was hard sometimes for them to understand what's good for them as opposed to the feminists. They're inclined to go down the line because they've been brainwashed by feminists. The first year I was on the DNC, in 1979, I set up the Black Affairs department to organize blacks, financed through the DNC. The National Women's Caucus within the DNC tried to get me to join, but I said no. I sweated so much blood to change them before—there was so much racism in the women's caucus. The feminists had a women's department that didn't have any women of color. They wanted to knock out the Black Affairs department, because it was competing for budget.

We had a black and labor caucus within the DNC. By having the support of one or the other, the feminists couldn't get a damn thing through the DNC. Then we got the Hispanic caucus, and that made it even harder for them to get things passed without us.

In my case, I know I was a power to deal with, within the black and labor caucus. There were a lot of women pretty green-eyed about that. I had helped change the power structure in the DNC, and I was there, waiting to have the feminists' shots come down on me.

Look, at the Black Affairs department, we registered over seven million voters—which Jesse Jackson took credit for later on. But us, the DNC, we had two full-time staffers involved in that.

> It looked so good to Jesse that he started running all over the country taking credit for it. That was okay with me. What did bother me was how he messed up the works for Walter Mondale in 1984. He made Mondale accept Gerry Ferraro on the ticket, and I didn't like that much. My choice was [U.S. Senator] Ernest Hollings, a good old Southern man who had a respectable record on labor and civil rights and human rights. And he's from the Carolinas. He could have swept across the southern part of the United States and taken that vote. Jesse didn't understand that at all.
>
> I can understand why young people would support him once they'd heard him talk. He's like Wellstone. He talks all those basic issues, but without any pragmatism about how you're going to put them in operation. Jesse said the right thing at least 50 percent of the time. But a person like me has to have both—someone who's principled enough on the issues, and also can win. (CP)

Paul Wellstone and I are both lucky to be alive. We were on the DNC together, and we fought like cats and dogs. The big fight we had was being on a small farmers committee chaired by Senator Tom Harkin of Iowa. He ran against me. As the vote was taking place, I remember thinking, oh, a tree grows in Brooklyn. There's Paul Wellstone jumping up and down trying to be a dirt farmer!

I won by some devious kinds of ways. I took a black woman educator, a state senator, and a farmer, threw her up and backed out of the way, and she won by one vote. I just felt coming from Minnesota, Iowa, we should be very broad about representation, for women and people of color, all those things together. I didn't realize Paul wanted to be a senator at the time; this was the eighties, remember, before he won that Senate seat in 1990.

Paul is pretty good, though. He's got guts—he can stand up and make a lot of noise. I voted for him every time, but I didn't jump and down and make a lot of noise about my undying support.

I just felt like there's a lot of things he could do. I think with the noise he's making, and the smartness he seems to have when he wants to be counted, he could support employment programs at the national level all the way. I'm not going to spell that out to you word for word, but if you remember all the speeches of Mario Cuomo about quality education and training, not only was Mario doing it, but one of his sons, Andrew, is doing it now as Secretary of Housing and Urban Development. Those are some of the basic things I'd like to see Wellstone do more of. I realize he's not been appointed a secretary, but senators are very strong people.

Paul's tried to be nice to me ever since that DNC affair. It's hard for me to perjure myself. He just didn't have to run for that seat—some local feminists put him up just to knock me off.

They finally got me off the DNC in 1988. You know I'm a hard numbers person, so I'll tell you this: at the 1988 Democratic state convention, I was beaten for my seat by nineteen votes—if I'd have gotten ten votes turned around, I could have won. I felt I'd done pretty well, out of a group of three thousand delegates, with everything they were saying about me.

A group of Minnesota women decided to find someone to run against me for the DNC at the state convention. Jackie Cherryhomes, who is now president of the Minneapolis City Council, was very involved in that, and Linda Higgins, who's now in the state senate, she called herself the manager of it. The woman they ran against me was Bea Underwood. I don't want to put Bea down, but she didn't know nearly as much about politics and labor as I did.

Age was a big part of the whispering campaign. I don't want to say I wasn't feeling old. I remember after the 1980 Africa trip, all of the unions traveled up to Duluth for a big rally. We were trying to demonstrate the strength of labor at a B&K rally up in International Falls, to stop them from using nonunion workers on a project. We just marched and carried banners. Danny Gustafson, who was president of the AFL-CIO at the time, said at the rally, "I don't know how long she's been around, but I've been looking at her for sixty years!" He himself was coming up on sixty at the time.

I kid about it, but I was seventy-five then, I just started to feel tired a little bit. I could run and jump until that time. I had sixty-five years of driving up and down streets every day, since I was nine—in Lakeville.

At seventy-five, I kept on working at the shop and on campaigns; this was just a year or so after Van White. I was used to carrying material around to headquarters, to candidates. I made it a point to learn the bus schedule real well so that I could do that.

The point is, even in 1988, at eighty-two or -three, I could run rings around my opponents mentally—I'm not bragging. They took me out, they said, for being too old. I would just throw it back at them—give them all examples of older white women with comparable jobs in policy in education and opportunity. People like Lillian Le Sueur, who was very old when she was making policy, grandiosely, for the DFL. Lillian might have been closer to ninety. But when I spoke to the convention, I spoke in generalities about myself as I always did. I didn't talk about the whispering campaign.

There were other whispers—that I was not really pro-choice, a lot of that stuff. It was not hard to beat me when there were a lot of snakes. They tried to beat me in 1984, tried to get even with me, but I used my union power. But I didn't ask the unions again in '88.

See, this all happened at that very same convention I launched my scholarship program in Minnesota—I simply took the brochures and passed them out to delegates. I sent a lot of brains and ears and eyes up at the sky. People would say, what is this? She never told us about that! We had a big dinner fund-raiser after that convention, a big announcement of the scholarship.

I knew my scholarship was coming up and I didn't want to spread myself too thin, supportwise. I wanted to keep as many people as possible united for the bigger goal of getting education for all. [The Nellie Stone Johnson Scholarship program, established in 1988, awards $500 to $2,500 annually, for up to four years, to minority union members and their families pursuing bachelor's and master's degrees within the Minnesota State College and University system.]

With the scholarship, I had a new reason to keep going, but after Bea won, I said to the community of color in north and south Minneapolis, I didn't lose, you lost. What did they lose? My loss upset a lot of equal opportunity progress. It upset a national scholarship program.

It would be fifty times as big, if not for feminists. I was trying to organize every state that had a big union presence to set up a fund just like the one we have in Minnesota. I knew which states had a heavy population of labor and minorities, because I had been on the DNC. Since I was not on the DNC, how could I organize other state committees like Minnesota? They couldn't knock me out in Minnesota—I was still on local committees.

Unfortunately, my loss was about window dressing. See, I know that's how people see me sometimes—I've had so much of that. I know people sometimes look up at me when I'm on a podium, or on some committee, and think, "She's there just because she's a black face."

I know when that happens. I do it anyway. It gives me an opportunity to sound off about my political and philosophical beliefs. I don't know if I want to acknowledge this or not, but when I became a candidate for the vice president of Local 665, I knew I was window dressing—but I wanted that vote on the board! They expected a token, but I turned out to be an activist animal! That helped me when I later ran for citywide office.

It's not hard to understand where people are coming from once you are in a political position. You just pay attention to how people vote and you know where people are coming from. When they trot you out, even if they expect you to be window dressing, it means they owe you—if you're smart enough to demand collection! In this case, a lot of ladies thought I had too much clout precisely because I wasn't window dressing *enough*.

The other thing that gets me about these so-called feminists is that they had set themselves up as power brokers, but they were not that political. They were not the most down-to-earth people in the

DFL feminist caucus, like others in the DFL who knew what it meant to do the job, real organizing.

————

In 1974, liberal suburbanite Joan Growe, elected to the Minnesota legislature with a group of feminists two years earlier, decided to move up to secretary of state. She held the post for six terms, before retiring in 1999.

————

I remember campaigning for Joan Growe when she first started out. This isn't a violent story. We were at the YWCA, some cheese-and-crackers thing to plan her convention run for secretary of state. There was a big argument with her feminist friends about when to announce her candidacy—play coy. I'm not about that. People were trying to assume knowledge of when to make the announcement, when to register folks as supporters.

I wanted her announcement to be there when people opened up the paper the next day. I knew if we waited until these so-called political advisers decided to stop dickering, it might be too late.

I had read the political situation at the time. Lou DeMars was my council member from the Fifth Ward. Remember, we would tussle over Van White down the road. Well, at that time, he would put me on any committee I wanted to be on—that was the relationship we had. I knew in the back of my mind that if Joan didn't get right in, Lou might. I just insisted we do it. So finally, Joan called the *Minneapolis Star Tribune,* told them she was in, and that was the first announcement.

Even though Joan Growe was a strong feminist, she was not one to go out and rip off her bra. A lot of feminists assert themselves on everything—right, wrong, indifferent. I assert myself, but I never saw myself with my bra off—even though I used to skinny-dip in the creek when I was a kid! I think at one time burning bras was a real political statement, but my causes are not that physical—employment, health care, housing, and education for everybody. It just seemed foolish to me that something that gave people comfort, health, or vanity was something you would try to make a policy out of. For me and the candidates I work with, there are no clever games. I'm a hard-nosed pol. I know what I see out there and I have pretty good vision.

The role of women in the union movement is exactly what it was in the general society: we are trailing men, subservient to men. There's got to be more hard work done by women there—I never expect anything to be handed to anyone, and I think my life proves that.

But if women think labor is unrepresentative of their concerns today, they're crazy because they don't understand history. Most women in my day came out of a home where some man was a member of the union. That elevated them financially to the standpoint where they could go to college, get an education, and fight for their rights. If you can't appreciate where you came from, how smart are you, really?

Chapter 25

Education

I think the best education on race for the ordinary person was in the 1950s and '60s, with the beatniks and later the hippies. I remember, I was working at the Wilsons', and Mr. Wilson said, what in the world are those people thinking about? He would talk about how those hippies had to take a bath and cut their hair. I thought to myself, he doesn't know what's going on philosophically. They're talking about the natural right of human beings to be treated as human beings. They spoke good words.

When you get in a class with traditional and nontraditional students you hear this. That's one reason I love the state college system so—lots of different people, less classism.

In 1987, Rudy put me on the state college board, which was then automatically folded into the MnSCU board. [The Minnesota State College board oversees several institutions of higher learning outside the University of Minnesota system. The board later became known as the Higher Education board and the Minnesota State College and University system, or MnSCU.]

Rod Searle, the former Republican Speaker of the House, and myself as the wild DFLer came on at the same time, and you couldn't have had a stranger combination. I liked Rod; he was a very honorable person.

There was no argument, no discussion between Rudy and me. I decided one day that was my job. I told him that's the job I wanted, and he knew my background and that was it. Rudy worked like that with his friends.

I did have to go before the legislature to get OK'd, though. There was a committee in the state senate, which was chaired by Jim Pehler out of St. Cloud. It started out real tough. They came at me—I remember the exact words Jim said. He said, "Nellie, I've known you for years, seen you around, and most of your activities deal with the inner city, bringing it down to inner-city things."

I said, "Oh, Senator, then you don't know me too well. Part of my history—I need to tell you—is for years, every morning I got up and milked fifteen cows, and that amounted to thirty cows a day. I could tell you the whole thing if you want to hear it." Jim Pehler threw up his hands and laughed and said, "That's enough, that's enough. You've got the vote, you're on." He didn't even take the vote, he just looked around—maybe they nodded, or there was some secret vote I didn't see. I was a little nervous, I'll admit, even sweating. But *boom,* I was approved.

I had a vision of doing exactly what I did with this—moving through in the community, having a little respect from the community beyond being vice president of Local 665 or the Minnesota Culinary Council.

I pushed for the same things on the board that I always did: I tried to maintain good wages and conditions for the employees, and get them to understand that good-quality education was for the normal person. Most of it came through the economic side. I worked hard to keep tuition down—lobbying, being a political animal was a big part of what I did. I just called my MnSCU lobbyist the other day, just the other day, to see what do. I'm going to the AFL-CIO convention, to promote people in the congressional districts for the new board coming up.

I had to be that political animal on the politics that drove the economics. When my term ended in 1988, I wanted to be reappointed, but I didn't want to be reappointed by Arne Carlson. To a certain extent, I didn't want him to be the person I was beholden to. I didn't want to be that brand of conservative that would have pushed nonequality right down the line. Despite some of the women saying he did good here and there, he didn't give a damn about women, black, and minorities. Why didn't he put a lot of money into higher education? I always argued with my feminist friends. If you're so concerned about the economic discrepancy between women's and men's wages, then he should have done more for education for all.

That high tuition is ruining it for ordinary families, and that includes a larger group of white students, and almost all Native Americans and blacks. People always seem to forget the fact that more white students get hit by that economic thing than minorities by racial discrimination. Because there are more whites. You can't even talk about what education should be until you have fair access to it.

I also had to be that political animal because it was such an anti-labor board. I was probably the only person on there that understood those contracts. I think at one time, we had twenty-one subdivisions of economics on that board for things we were writing into contracts.

Now a place like Metro State is genuinely diverse, but there's a lot of building that went down using money that should have been spent on real education. The St. Paul campus is too expensive, they had to float another bond. I wanted a campus at Penn and Washington in north Minneapolis—the old Control Data Institute. It was logical and was set up for education. But we had these women on the board, they wanted nothing to do with north Minneapolis. The people there, there's a psychological myth—that it's so much safer and nicer somewhere else other than anywhere in North Minneapolis.

1995: Nellie at Ninety

In Bloomington, in a fine hotel
where once Nellie could only
wash the dishes or clean the rooms
for women's wages, we gather
to celebrate and honor her work
and her life. The room is bright
and warm with the glow of
good friends and good deeds done.

But behind those kitchen doors,
or downstairs in the laundry,
or across the road cleaning
some green office building,
there is a woman named Francesca
who works part time and has no health care,
whose son is sick and whose daughter
has disappeared into the streets.
There is a man named Chen
who wants to marry a woman
named Lien, who is saving to take
her first course at Metro State.

There is Cheryl May, going home tonight
on 38th Street to take care of her mother
and her grandfather, who sits too near
the radiator in their two rooms
above the used furniture store,
trying to get warm.

Wait, Nell, wait. Don't leave.
Don't go yet. I'm almost done.
OK, OK, I understand.
Someone give her that stack of pamphlets.
Jerry, pass her those signature cards.
And, Chris, give her that scholarship brochure
for Chen to take to Lien.

I know, I know. Time again to get down to business,
for Nellie at ninety, and for each of us,
blessed by her long life, and by her love.

Goodnight, Nellie, my dear friend.
Give 'em hell!

From "Nellie at Ninety"
(Robert L. Carothers 1995)

One of the things I am proudest of is my scholarship within MnSCU, the Nellie Stone Johnson Scholarship program. The idea is now twelve or so years old. I think the idea was brewing, beginning to ferment or generate itself, two years prior to that. I had talked to someone, a power in education that understood what the hell I was talking about. This was Robert Carothers, the president of Southwest State.

I'd been beating the officialdom up about having a minority scholarship. The country was pretty much into inequalities there in the 1980s. That was sweeping the land, killing off opportunity, including the way to true equality through quality education.

When Robert Carothers was our system chancellor, I would call him every other week. I was so concerned about school aid, especially to black and Native American students, two groups almost left completely out. And I wanted to help the families of union members, as a part of my union history. There was nothing to the political extent anyone was doing. But then unions and the educational establishment got together, with the help of the DFL Party, and began raising money in my name.

I tell you, I would like to thank, number one, Chancellor Carothers, who is now the president of the University of Rhode Island. Then, for helping me over the hurdle, to recognize labor and the need for people of color to learn, I would like to mention the name of Dan Gustafson, head of the state AFL-CIO. He was one of the toughest rednecks around, but he understood the need to read and write and be trained. I think we need to periodically mention the state AFL-CIO federation, especially the president, Bernie Brommer, and Dave Roe prior to Danny. Also Bill Peterson, who is retiring officially as a vice president.

You don't know what a thrill it is to see class after class of my scholarship people built up. There are people like this young man from Forest Lake, he's still in the making. Timkins is his name, and he goes to Mankato State. He called me just the other day and we talked. He's going to reapply for next year. He's into some kind of engineering, into business, but I guess the reason I'm going on about him is that everything he does, every vision he has, is about clearing up the areas that are most polluted for people of color. He's concerned with the Native American and black communities, because they're the ones treated the worst environmentally in the whole country. You ask me who will pick up the gauntlet, you can't help but be moved by young people such as him.

On May 26, 1995, at the age of eighty-nine, Nellie was awarded an honorary Doctor of Humane Letters degree in humanities by St. Cloud State University.

That degree meant a lot to me, because everything I'd worked for all my life, for the equality of people in education, in the economic field, was folded into what that honorary degree was all about. I also felt very good about being associated and recognized with one of my best friends, one of the people I respected the most in the DFL structure, Walter Mondale.

I tell you, I worked harder for that honorary degree than most people worked for their earned degree, and I'm including doctors! If anyone wants to think I'm a country bumpkin who doesn't know anything about education, they're crazy. I know the whole structure, shall we say, and I've got the paper to prove it.

I didn't cry on the platform when I got my degree, but when I got the word it was coming down, I choked to myself—I like to go through those miseries by myself, then come out and have people think I never went through those agonies at all.

When he told me, the president of St. Cloud said, "I've got a great big favor to ask. You will be receiving this degree, but we don't have a speaker at our commencement." I thought, if good things don't keep falling on my head! I had a lot to tell people about why they needed their education.

— Chapter 26 —

Racism Today

Occasionally white people who try to be nice people will say they accept me, but I always tell them, my question is, do I accept you? I'm not trying to be rude, but I want to let them know that it's racism, even if it's unintentional, to put yourself in the superior position over someone else. It takes two to make real acceptance.

I think when you go into a truly religious area, you have a great sense of right and wrong. I say truly religious because religion is one area where I see major inequality. I hate to use this in the book, but if you look at every church at eleven on Sunday morning, you sometimes find the most immorality. Discrimination is rampant. Oh, sure, you can attend services. Someone might shake your hand, and gush over you, but being allowed to worship on a consistent basis, you're not welcome.

My dad used to tell a story. There was a man on the steps of the church, and along came another man and asked why he couldn't get in. This second man said he should get in so he could worship. And the first person said, "I'm God, and I've been trying to get in there for years!"

The thing is, how do you deal with that religious intolerance? That tends to strengthen the right, which wants to divide people against themselves. I've never really settled that one, which is why I still have very mixed feelings about religion.

Is there still racism today, with all the gains that have been made? In everything. I have a very simple answer for those who say that we've gone too far, and now there's all this "reverse discrimination." With the big discrepancies in education and employment, there can *never* be reverse discrimination. Most big companies are still lily-white if they are anything.

People cannot be a hundred percent discriminated against if they have a job, decent training, and an education. If someone doesn't get a job, it's the power structure's fault.

Some paper called me up about violence in the so-called ghetto the other day. I said, look at the corporate towers. That's where the real violence happens, that's where people are denied jobs.

People would have the nerve to say to me, "I didn't know someone as skilled as you came out of the black community." I say to them, "I could even build you a house," kind of flipping off to them.

It pains me to say this, but part of this attitude is hardened by who the teachers are and what environment they are turned out in. What these so-called qualified teachers have done with their certification process is put whoever makes it through the third degree, but they don't have the cultural background, the scholarly, academic background, to understand what teaching in the black community is.

The people who are talking about discrimination in education—they're right. There are so many teachers in kindergarten through twelfth grade who are not qualified to teach, and nobody wants to address that. I tried to get the labor caucus going on reform in the Minnesota Federation of Teachers five or six years ago, but it only demonstrated that we just couldn't get it going. The younger teachers in the middle schools, they are more emotional that something could be done out there.

I practically kicked in the door to see the vice president of the Minnesota Federation of Teachers a few years ago to talk to her about it. The teachers and their leadership certainly expressed a desire for higher education for all. They say it's the system's fault. Well, I do believe it goes all the way from instructors to the boards. I mean, first you have to get by the human resources departments of the public school boards. They hire these people. Teachers become that way—racist—if they get the OK from their board, or their bureaucracy. Whether it's right or not, they have their ideas of what to do and what politics to play to keep blacks and American Indians second-class citizens.

I have always assumed my own responsibility—and that was my whole card with teachers: assume responsibility. I had a built-in knowledge of what has become quite a cliché—personal responsibility. It's the right thing to do.

I was very upset with the teachers' reaction. Frustration set in. It doesn't happen to me very often, thank goodness. The teachers, they're very concerned about their jobs, but there's no political concern about stiffening up their spine. I remember I used to think that if I hadn't been fired, there was something wrong with me! I had to remind them, some of us peons were out getting contracts for teachers—and if we hadn't, they would not have had a contract!

There are definitely some well-intentioned things that have hurt. Busing was very harmful to the black community. My dad drove a van to get all the kids to the Hinckley schools. I never liked busing, even when I was riding the bus myself.

Anyway, this is not giving black people a crutch—these are about the tools we need. I don't have to be starving to death to be told that I might be hungry.

Some people within the black community accuse me of being way out there on educational change. You could interview a hundred people on Thirty-eighth and Fourth in south Minneapolis, or a hundred at Plymouth and Penn in north Minneapolis, and they would have a good idea of what's going wrong in public schools. I actually did that—went through with interviewing a hundred people on those spots, and I never got one argument that we needed to do more focusing on employment and education. So I said, can I speak for you? It was kind of a loaded question.

There has to be a good education. You have to analyze this. It has to be the right kind of education—an adherence to the rights and wrongs of how to treat human beings. Public education in Minnesota has been indicative of that.

Part of what's happening today is that young people are not radical, but the basic human philosophy sticks with them. There's been so much success in the DFL Party—look what's happened in education, as messed up as it can get. At least it's not restricted to the chosen few, though there are many who are not getting what they should.

I worry that we'll change in the wrong direction, though. I remember arguing with an officer of the Minnesota Federation of Teachers in opposition to vouchers, tax dollars for private education. She was saying this stuff privately, but it became apparent that in her mind people get a better education in the private sector. This was an officer of a public teachers union! You'd die if I told you what her office was—very high up. This issue is important because good public schooling is important to equality for jobs. And do you really think public schooling will get better if we let private schools take more of the best students with tax dollars helping them?

It's not just about access to education, but what kind of education you get. Up to a point, the whole meaning of liberal arts has be across-the-board education of what's right and wrong for all people. A lot of racial minorities don't know the real finances and politics of history—the real role racism has played in perpetuating the system—but they have a degree! People have to come out with their liberal arts all together, figure out the financial and economic impact of labor, how to influence the education and health of children. Our educational system has to be wide and inclusionary, and that's what I have worked for. We've made it more equal, but it's not equal, not by a long shot.

Part of it is our own fault. All over town, the so-called black organizations are a bunch of middle-class people and superliberals who just don't have the best interests of the basic community at heart. You only have to look at what they now call the Hollman projects, which the middle class and the superliberals wanted to blow up!

The Hollman case is named after Lucy Hollman, a public housing tenant in the federally subsidized Sumner-Olson public housing projects in north

Minneapolis. In 1992, the Minneapolis branch of the NAACP, and seven-teen plaintiffs organized by Minneapolis Legal Aid, including Hollman, filed suit against federal, state, and local agencies, alleging that Minneapolis public housing services perpetuated racial segregation. In 1995, the parties settled, agreeing to tear down 770 of Hollman's 988 units. In return, the federal government agreed to fund 900 Section 8 certificates, which theo-retically allow recipients to move anywhere where a landlord accepts the vouchers—though many don't. The federal government also agreed to fund the 770 units of replacement housing by 2001.

———————

You don't have to be black and over 90 years old to appreciate the im-portance to black heritage of the shameful pile of muck Jennifer Vogel exposed in her excellent article on the northside public hous-ing land grab, a scheme devised by the City of Minneapolis, HUD, the Legal Aid Society, and of all people, the Minneapolis NAACP. But maybe it helps.

I joined the Minneapolis NAACP in 1934 and was elected to the Board of Directors in 1938. I paid my dues faithfully year after year with money, work, commitment, and love. Almost 50 years ago I be-came an NAACP lifetime member. Now, with the *Hollman* lawsuit settlement, I find that we have fought the wrong battles, won false victories, that we—the black masses of Minneapolis—need to be "deconcentrated," spread out, so that we don't poison each other. And our land, we need to give that back to our social betters!

For over 50 years, black people have had their babies, raised their families, and buried their dead in the near north area of Minneapolis. Now, before I meet my maker, I see what it all comes down to: the lib-erals selling out the only black land we have ever known in Minne-apolis to a bunch of development interests, with black leaders from the mayor to our community organizations falling into line.

Shame on the Minneapolis NAACP for participating in this ter-rible attack on our community. . . .

. . . Have all the good black people lost their voices? Stand up before it's too late for black children, grandchildren, and great-grandchildren. (Nellie Stone Johnson, letter to the editor, *City Pages*, November 29, 1995)

———

By mid-1999, only a few vouchers and replacement housing units had been built for the poor; meanwhile, city officials promoted a rebuilding program for the "Hollman site" that included only 25 percent public housing. In the midst of a growing shortage of affordable housing during economic boom times, protests erupted over the net loss of affordable housing.

———

I need to put that out when people of color are committing suicide on the Hollman decree. You can't support people business-wise and political-wise who are so contrary of the basic policy of the organization. You can't take an organization noted for equality of people, and do this, and I'm talking about the NAACP. They supported tearing down housing from every poor, Native American, black, or Asian in Minneapolis. Now they're saying they need more housing, so I was right.

At the time this demolition was first being touted, I said why not rehabilitate them—do what was done with the project in 1935–36 when it was built up from scratch? I was there in 1935, when there were a lot of meetings to get Sumner-Field [the actual name of the buildings covered by the Hollman decree] through, to get *more* housing for our people, not less.

Everyone calls them the projects now, but sixty years ago, they had a lot of education in the projects, a lot of people had jobs there, black and white. My union business agents, neither of them black, had large families and raised them there just fine. There's no reason we can't restore that type of plan.

Soon, there will be nothing there. On the task forces, it seemed like the opponents of keeping that housing up had their act together; I could do nothing short of killing myself to stop it.

The so-called concentration of poverty is nothing new, and if people want to progress, they do what they have to do, stick together, to get ahead. The Eastern Seaboard was taken over by the Irish; people like Tip O'Neill, Kennedys, a lot of the Italians worked the same way. They don't move out, they move forward. The concerns of poor people don't make any difference anymore.

The weakness in the black community is this: the middle class that people like me helped build, the black middle class, aren't like the Irish and Italians. They knew how to take their people down the alley to better economic opportunity, but we do not. There's a lack of political understanding and the get-up-and-go to have an impact on our own economics.

Part of the reason why there is still so much racism is because of a lack of political activity by people who the racism is used against! Jews have the Anti-Defamation League. At one time, the NAACP was what blacks had. Not only am I a life member of the NAACP, but I've got a lifetime training in education. I did twenty-six consecutive years on the Minneapolis branch executive committee. What has happened is the enemies of affirmative action have gotten on the board. The NAACP tried to take some strong stands, but they were upset by people who were part of the power structure, and who, by wanting to please power rather than fight the system, have become the enemies of affirmative activists. The black members of the organization don't understand the deviousness of the people on the board making policy. I am a life member of the NAACP, and I do not part with five hundred dollars easily [the cost of a lifetime membership], so I just about fainted when they pushed that Hollman suit through.

With many people in the black community, their work influences their philosophy. Take, for instance, in education, I see it very vividly. Some people who work for TCF bank, like the black Republican Peter Bell, they never talk about how discrimination happens in the black community. They keep people in the slave mind. That's one reason I started the scholarship—I knew what would happened to black students unless they knew what slavery was about. The average black kid never thinks about the economic consequences of slavery. They couldn't tell you what the Civil War was about!

I once went to this workshop at the National Business Machines Corporation. The NAACP was part of a sponsoring group, or so they put out on their brochure. They had a guy on their board who was a white redneck businessman. He said, we will get you a full scholarship, but at the end of it, we want you educated in our mold—the slave mold. I knew one of their vice presidents, he traveled with Fritz Mondale, and he just said yes, that's true.

You might be surprised after everything I've said that I don't agree with people who say Minnesota is just as racist as other places, just more quiet about it. I do know where the racism is, but I won't say this is a predominantly racist state. That seems like the fashionable thing for people to say these days, because there is still a lot of racism, no doubt about it. It's out there. But I feel Minnesota is definitely a less racist place, and it may be somewhat because of me and my family being involved in Minnesota for over a century. At least we talk about it here—the political and educational avenues to make changes.

The laws and regulations are there if people want to work hard at enforcing it. It's like the Constitution—the laws that are there may look nice, but they don't matter much if you don't work as hard to enforce 'em as they did to make 'em.

I blame the whole power structure for criminal justice racism. The power structure is not in the hands of the county attorney, the Urban League, or the MEA. It's in the Chamber of Commerce, the whole corporate structure. I tell labor, you're a victim of the same structure that we blacks are, too. The same thing is happening to the young labor worker, the young white worker, about their wages, working conditions, political power—I just jump up and down about it. I say, hold hands, what hurts one hurts others. I learned that very early in life.

It's not a hard argument in my mind. I think parts of the general society are often corrupt, biased against any kind of betterment of working-class people. I have young groups of blacks ready to knock me down and kill me when I talk about labor, but I say, look at the people who want modern-day slavery and look at the antiunion people—neither of them wants you to get a good education.

A lot of poor people once argued against Social Security because they saw a lot of black people being beneficiaries, so of course, they didn't want it, even though it would have helped them. I understand those shenanigans. Look, the people who were manipulating those poor folk knew exactly what they were doing—big businesspeople who didn't want to pay those taxes in the first place.

There is more ability to direct, to manipulate poor white people and poor black people today because they've been able to put a big black mark on the heads of big unions. Look at the United Auto Workers, which has some of the most powerful black leaders in the country. Of course, it's not just on the head of unions, but the total organization. Unions are not any good, they're Mafia-ridden, they spend taxpayer money—what you're really doing is calling education and health care frivolous.

I know everything's not perfect with unions—they are a part of society. One of the big deterrents to a real movement among people of color is AFSCME. That's the biggest block among labor these days. We've treaded sidewalks for the recognition of public employees, but they are not doing their share for the rights of minorities or to get more minorities into unions. It's like, they got theirs . . .

They are not recognizing caucuses within themselves which could get opportunities for people—they should recognize black caucuses, for example. Back then, when we were getting going, it seemed like there were a hundred and fifty progressive, liberal caucuses within Local 665 for people of color. I'm going to a conference of black trade unionists here in Minneapolis—here's Resolution Thirteen I'm going to propose—defend affirmative action. Well, of course.

I haven't ever changed my mind about affirmative action. Politically, people who make the argument that equal opportunity and affirmative action aren't the same thing aren't as intelligent as they should be. You have to have affirmative action to get there. If people believe this really isn't a racist society, and that we don't have to do something to include more people of color, they're crazy.

We've just got to recognize that black women and Native Americans are the two groups at the low end of the totem pole. It's a good one when people say we've done enough for them. That's said by people who have gotten what *they* want out of the market.

One of the things that gave me hope recently is when [Federal Reserve chairman] Alan Greenspan said if anyone in the corporate world believed in racism, they might as well go out of business. If I live long enough to see that day, it will be a great thing.

I have seven grandnephews and nieces in college. When I was speaking at River Falls last year, one of the students asked my grandnephew Kyle Olson Patterson, who goes to school there, if he had ever faced racism. Kyle's skin is whiter than most people's skin. I knew the undercurrent in the questioner's mind—they wonder how in the world someone like him could experience racism. They don't realize that regardless of what color you are, if you have one drop of black blood, you're black. It doesn't work the other way, and I know because I have several drops of white blood!

That kid in Wyoming who was killed because he was gay [Matthew Shepard, whose murder gained national attention after he was tied to a fencepost and tortured to death], his case is no different than that of blacks. My nephew Kyle, he has friends that look black, they've been friends for years. He was actually stopped by cops out West who said what are you doing with kids like this, and he immediately said right back—he's such a sweet child—because they're my friends. That's all it is. That shows you the racism that's still out there.

— Chapter 27 —

The Nineties

Somebody asked me . . . what I thought was going to happen
when we founded the DFL Party. I said I thought by now we
would have taken over the whole country. And I did. At the
time, I thought our politics were so good, so pure, so equal-
ity-minded that it didn't make any difference where we
went, people would flock to us. That hasn't been the case.

(CP)

In my late eighties, I cut my hours down and was only open three days
a week. Nothing else I could do. I finally shut down my business in '97.
I began to move myself out. I was in business on my own thirty-four
years, twelve to fourteen hours per day. By the time I quit, everybody
knew Nellie. The businessmen, they all knew me—one jeweler called
me Queen of the Mall.

I was getting tired doing it, and I'm sorry to say it was getting hard
to get employees and train 'em from scratch. Also, the building I was
in was not that good: 920 Nicollet—in the old Meyer's Arcade. Just a
few months ago I got my last stuff out, they tore it all down for some
fancy development.

This thing is getting so bad on the black perspective—the continuing racism geared to the black community. This is how twenty-three
white students in Littleton get killed by racism—one hater gets a gun
and goes after black people, and twenty-three white students die. The

basic thing, what I'm saying, and have been trying to say for a hundred years to people, is what comes over the back of black people is going to come to you. Those Littleton killers didn't want these black kids in school, and they didn't want the athletic programs given to black students, and the other thing is that some blacks were making too much money and becoming more professional. There is so much racism out there today, it frightens the hell out of me—it borders on the 1930s with anti-Semitism.

I'll admit, the overall attitude of the family farmers looks pretty pessimistic and dismal. They feel like they're caught in the same stuff labor is, the corporate world is buying them up. Look at the mortgages of family farmers—when they go down, six corporations are there to gobble them up.

The people in power *still* don't want to recognize that these attitudes exist—they would have to confront all the racism that benefits *them* in the rest of their lives. I think that particular type of co-op like my dad's creamery has passed, but I think a different type of co-op venture could survive. I'm not sure what it is—I'm looking for a visionary just like everyone else. Something like that has got to happen over again. You just can't have a few at the top usurping ninety percent of the money. There are too many workers, too many people trying to grasp a living from forty acres and mule.

Did I waste my time doing farm organizing? I should say not! It's part of the educational process, of making things better for people then, now, and in the future. It's too bad that you have to do it again, each generation, to get where our parents were, trying to get some equality, some stability for the family farmers. I know that small farmers are not doing so well, and hence the merchants in those small towns are not doing so well, either. It's more than economics—there's got to be some stability in how you treat people.

If family farmers die off and there are corporate farms, God help the United States, we'll have no U.S. There is a certain philosophical thing—bigger farms take you to plantations, and that means more inequality of people. Some people may not think we'll go back to slavery, but this could be close to it. Individuals, especially workers, will lose power against the big overseer, in many ways. That's why unions happened. Look at this labor organization of the doctors they're talking about—people simply have to have some organizing unit to speak for them en masse instead of doing things, negotiating, individually. It's ironic, because all good health programs came through the labor movement, probably put a lot of money in those doctors' pockets.

What happens on a political level if family farms go away? I've been a little fearful of that for a long time. Farmers, to a great extent, have not had the class divisions, despite differences in land ownership, or they have not bought into the class divisions of the urban society. It gets back to inequality of people, a lack of humanity. Things are worse off for all.

Of course, everyone is not truly represented. We've got a lot of piecemeal stuff—the community of women, the community of color, a lot of factions. The biggest thing is that there's not the kind of cohesiveness. Say, for instance, equality for women: fifty percent don't vote as Democrats or Republican, but vote as women—you have to have a tight organization. We damn near got hung up as on the abortion issue. I was one of the first people that slid out of that thing because if the abortion issue, pro-life or pro-choice, was taking out a number of good politicians, who is doing the fundamental work on good jobs and equality? We should just take that abortion issue out of politics right now.

I think the DFL is still more in touch with the ordinary people. Right now, I think their future DFL is so-so, but philosophically sometimes they just don't do it. They have not put in rules or regulations for true equality in the school systems, or pushed for more equality for family farmers.

There are simply too many pockets of conservatism in the DFL, too many MBAs who determine how things go, from the point of view of the business faction. They're making rules and regulations to the point where the legislature is playing around to give more power to the private sector than the public sector. I can tell you the private sector is the root of racism, the determining factor on whether people are discriminated against.

The Republicans are worse off. Some people might be surprised by that, but unless you go where the bulk of the people are, how are you going to win? That's what came out of the New Deal, just fundamental policies that benefited the most people, not your Chambers of Commerce or the wealthy only.

I said these days, people have to justify helping other people, and I think that's the influence of the private sector. I tell you, I hope to God nobody has lost the feeling that what is good for their neighbor will not be good for themselves. That's just the sort of feeling the conservative ruling class wants, to keep power without having to worry about organizing. People need to know about economic political history of how everyone got ahead. I don't think people are getting ahead right now. Nobody is doing the good, solid organizing and education to tell people where the real influence lies, with the private sector and the influence peddlers that are doing so well at their expense.

I think there is room for three or four parties. I'm the product of a third party, the Farmer-Labor Party. Nationally, the DFL Party became a third party, and I thought we did very well and produced damn good candidates. If the DFL keeps slipping, I think there could be another party today. What I see around the horn, with these special-interest groups so powerful, it may not take much. Minnesota is known for humane things. In the 1920s and '30s, we were known as the labor state, and then the organization of workers. Out of that came vacation programs, health programs, and lots of very humane programs. Civil and human rights. Special interests will toss much of that out the window.

In 1998, Minnesotans elected their first third-party governor in more than sixty years: the Reform Party's tough-talking, ex-pro wrestler Jesse Ventura. He pushed for tax rebates over new social spending, but also campaign finance reform, and offered a nearly libertarian social philosophy—against

---

I almost hate for it to be in print what I think of Jesse. I'm a Farmer-
Laborite, and *that* was a third party, and turned out to almost take
over the country. On Jesse, I wish he knew a little more and adhered to
cultural diversity. That's basically what I think of him.

He says he hires people for his staff without regard to race, color,
and creed. But his hiring did not denote that at all, and then, when he
met with a group of color who were concerned about this early in his
term, he basically said, "Get up off your butts and do something."
That's an insult—like people of color haven't.

I guess that hit me the hardest. I wasn't in that meeting when the
people of color met with him, but I understand there were blacks,
Native Americans, Asians, and he started talking about get yourself
trained, you're lazy, get off your butts, and repeated a lot of discrimination clichés about people of color. I think it's easy for Jesse to say he
hires without regard. That's like most white Minnesotans have said
over the years—get out and get an education, we will hire you. Then
they say, well, we will hire only skilled people, and deny people of color
the right to professions or education needed to have those kind of
skills. He can't find minority people in the whole state who are qualified? That doesn't make him look very smart.

Jesse has taken the words that he thinks to use, with his experience
of populism. He gets into that antigovernment kind of thing, but
then he turned around and I hear him use the very words that were
popular in the New Deal. I hear that coming out of both ends of
people sometimes—he's talking like that. He's got people coming and
going, and no one's caught on to him yet.

I didn't pay too much attention to that stuff he said in the campaign
about being a union member. It didn't impress me. He's kind of halfway in between on the labor movement. Unions are about protecting

people at every level of their operaion, and Jesse sounds like an I've-got-mine kind of person. I don't see him doing anything organizationally to help lift people up. The way he treated those people of color meeting with him, his retort did not speak well for unions. Unions are almost the backbone of the movement for equal opportunity for people of color. The black community, which is one hundred percent working class, has relied very heavily on the labor movement. If he was a real union man, he would understand that. But he seems to regard certain kinds of people as not part of his kind of populism, if you know what I mean.

On the education side of things, well, I keep going back to this, but the way he handled those people of color who met with him early in his term didn't speak too highly of his understanding. Even though he spent the money on elementary and secondary education, I think somebody close to him should tell him that K–12 education was the way to get to most people. You know so many things when you've worked in this political system as long as I have, you just know where things come off.

I do not think he is all the way sincere in his populism. If you don't talk to a big group of Minnesotans, that shows it.

You told me Paul Wellstone wonders whether Jesse has compassion. Paul and I may disagree on something, but not this.

You ask me who will pick up the gauntlet, and that's a tough one. I sincerely think it has to be labor-oriented people, and when I say labor, I say go with the platform of labor—nondiscrimination on the basis of race, creed, color, and gender, all of those things that make it impossible, at least on paper, to discriminate.

Thank God, the labor movement has not quit doing politics. The big corporate Chambers of Commerce, we have not quit locking horns with them. What keeps me going so vividly is people like the president of the national Chamber. Everything that pertained to humanity, they were in opposition to it, like health programs. It's about how you have to work politically against corporate people—they are not geared to humanity, but to the almighty dollar. It's a dismantling of good education, period, and good health programs.

I never feel defeated if there are two unorganized people out there—there's the possibility of them getting organized and educated about taking care of their health and family. And the basics of education, in order to give themselves a good way of life.

I'd tell organizations today to keep up the fight, to keep it down to earth on the equality of people. There's a certain degree of genderism, too, of course, people fighting the equality of gender.

As for my union friends, most are not grabbing ahold of the politics. You can make a candidate do the right thing. You groom them for their position. At a local and regional level, you groom their education, their public education. You threaten 'em and you talk to 'em and later, you do their PR work. You give them something to brag about later. That's a bit of what I did with Hubert.

If the unions and the political parties are going to live, they've got to get back to organizing for the rights of everyone, especially those hit by oppression. Even white-collar people are going to get hit by that eventually. Take the Newspaper Guild: they've come under pressure as papers want to contract out more work to people without health benefits, or to journalists at papers without unions.

The unions, they're attempting to organize again. That's a part of the total labor movement, of course. Everyone has to belong to a certain local, which is where it starts.

One thing I have learned in my life, especially the part spent in the union movement, is that anybody who believes in a change in the status quo is considered radical. There are people right now in Minneapolis who are protesting increased segregation in the schools that are doing what we did to create labor—meet and rally. Now they have to get active politically.

For all of humanity, the hope is that unions will be strong. I really don't know what will come to be. I want to see the philosophy of labor prevail because the basic philosophy is to feed people, put a roof over their heads, and provide a quality education. Some people read better than other people, and there's a certain philosophical thing on labor, some people are not reading it correctly. Nobody has to tell me about the numbers—the Central Labor Body in Minneapolis used to have 160,000 or 170,000 members, almost what the state does now. But the philosophical craving for labor is still there—better education, income enough to send your kids to school for a good education, quality food. Very simple things for humanity.

Remember when Hubert died, I said his legacy was to be remembered for what he did for ordinary people. The thing that I want to be sure to come out in my book is that I want the same thing for me. To be remembered for working for the family farmer and labor—the salt of the earth. Those are the ordinary people in the state of Minnesota.

Commencement Address by Nellie Stone Johnson
St. Cloud State University
May 26, 1995

Graduates, parents, relatives, and friends,

I am pleased to be here to share this day with you. A day that is a joyful day. A day that is the culmination of years of hard work. A day that is the culmination of many years of sacrifice and discipline by you and those who love and care about you.

Today, you receive a symbol of your education efforts.

The State University System and St. Cloud State have fulfilled their pact with you and their mission of providing quality education to all persons regardless of background or circumstances.

You have been given the tools—not a guarantee. Tools to achieve economic security, community status. Tools to make a difference.

The greatest tool you have been given is vision—you have always had a vision.

A vision through education has been honed, focused.

This vision, however, means nothing unless it is pursued, followed, turned into action.

Yes, your visions include economic security for family, success for yourself.

But this is hollow unless you strive to realize a shared vision for the community in which we live. You cannot be an educated island of people. You must and will interact with society and all its peoples.

You must as educated people be concerned about a society that:

- spends more on incarceration than education
- spends more on destruction than construction
- worries more about corporate profits than a decent wage
- has us believing that unemployment and signs of a slow economy are good
- puts people's classes and races against each other to prevent action for the common good.

You are educated. You have vision.

You have the ability and training to look beyond the sound bites, the film clips, the propaganda, the invitations to hate, the soaps that lead to inactivity.

Use this vision. Enhance this vision. Use your education for your good and the common good.

Pursue excellence.

Be truly educated men and women.

Bibliography

Books

Blegen, Theodore C. *Minnesota: A History of the State.* Minneapolis: University of Minnesota Press, 1963.

Clark, Clifford E., Jr. (ed.), *Minnesota in a Century of Change: The State and Its People since 1900.* St. Paul: Minnesota Historical Society Press, 1989.

Faue, Elizabeth. *Communities of Suffering and Struggle: Women, Men, and the Labor Movement in Minneapolis, 1915–1945.* Chapel Hill: University of North Carolina Press, 1991.

Holmquist, June D. (ed.). *They Chose Minnesota: A Survey of the State's Ethnic Groups.* St. Paul: Minnesota Historical Society Press, 1988.

Humphrey, Hubert H. *The Education of a Public Man: My Life and Politics.* Ed. Norman Sherman. Minneapolis: University of Minnesota Press, 1992.

Lass, William E. *Minnesota: A Bicentennial History.* New York: Norton, 1977.

McWilliams, Carey. *A Mask for Privilege: Anti-Semitism in America.* Boston: Little, Brown, 1948.

Ross, Carl (ed.). *Radicalism in Minnesota 1900–1960: A Survey of Selected Sources.* St. Paul: Minnesota Historical Society Press, 1994.

Oral History

Berman, Hy. Carl Ross interview: Twentieth-Century Radicalism in Minnesota Oral History Project. Transcript. St. Paul: Minnesota Historical Society.

Gilman, Rhoda, et al. Nellie Stone Johnson interview: Twentieth-Century Radicalism in Minnesota Oral History Project. Transcript. St. Paul: Minnesota Historical Society. (Cited in text as MHS.)

Ross, Carl. George Naumoff interview: Twentieth-Century Radicalism in Minnesota Oral History Project. Transcript. St. Paul: Minnesota Historical Society.

Periodicals

McWilliams, Carey. "Minneapolis: The Curious Twin." *Common Ground* (Autumn 1946).

Mengelkoch, Louise. Article on Nellie Stone Johnson. *Minnesota Women's Press* 2, no. 4 (May 27–June 9, 1986), 1, 8. (Cited in text as MWP.)

Perry, Steve. "The Good Fight: Nellie Stone Johnson's 70 Years in Minnesota Politics." *City Pages* (May 29, 1991). (Cited in text as CP.)